The Alhambra

ARCHITECTURE • HISTORY • MAPS • LEGENDS

Ediciones Miguel Sánchez

© *of this edition:* Ediciones Miguel Sánchez

Texts: Ana Sánchez *and* Ángel Sánchez
Except for monographs specifically identified with an (*)

Photography: Ángel Sánchez
Except for photographs specifically identified with an (**)

Drawings: Ana Campos *and* Carlos Quintanilla

Coordination: Ediciones Miguel Sánchez editorial team

Translation by: Robin Myers (STU traductores, s.l.)

Design and Layout: Susana Martínez Ballesteros

Prepress: Paperlitos

Printing: Gracor, s.l.

I.S.B.N.: 978-84-7169-138-5

Legal deposit: Gr-397/2014

(*) Rafael Hierro Calleja *The Muslim Peoples, Masters of al-Ándalus (711-1492)*, p. 18 • *The Catholic Monarchs, Architects of the Unity of the Spanish Kingdoms*, p. 52 • *Decoration and Ornamentation (I): Techniques, Resources and Decorative Elements of Islamic Architecture*, p. 108 • *Decoration and Ornamentation (II): Most Frequent Decorative Themes and Motifs*. "Epigraphic motifs," p. 142; "Plant motifs," p. 143.

Antonio Marín *Decoration and Ornamentation (II): Most Frequent Decorative Themes and Motifs*. "Geometric motifs," p. 144.

(**) Javier Algarra *View of Granada and the Sierra Nevada*, pp. 12 and 13 • *Court of the Myrtles, north portico*, p. 95 • *Chamber of Ambassadors*, p. 103 • *Chamber of Ambassadors*, p. 104 • *Ceiling of the Chamber of Ambassadors*, p. 105 • *Hall of the Kings*, p. 132 • *Steam Room*, pp. 166 and 167.

Ediciones Miguel Sánchez Archive *Lindaraja Viewpoint from the Hall of Two Sisters*, p. 141 • Bath of the *Sultan in the Immersion Room*, p. 169.

Guido Montañés *Corner of the Court of Machuca*, p. 83 • *The Palace of the Generalife and its surroundings*, pp. 216 and 217.

Miguel Sánchez *Column of the Court of the Lions*, p. 68 • *Detail of one of the nine open bedrooms along the Chamber walls*, p. 102 • *Paintings on leather in the Hall of the Kings*, pp. 134 and 135 • *Detail of the walls in the Rest Room*, p. 160 • *Rest Room*, pp. 164 and 165.

TO MIGUEL SÁNCHEZ (1921-1996)

Books contain life. Life that is born when a project develops,
transforming a dream into reality. Life shared by everyone who participates
in its creation, and life propagated and multiplied by every reader.

But the soul of a book is something more. It is the silent life that dwells
in the sensitivity of a publisher working in the shadows,
choosing the right paper, the suitable type, the evocative cover,
and the details that imprint a book with character, making it unique.

From 1951 to 1996, Miguel Sánchez, the creator of this publishing house,
knew how to imbue its books with the quality only attained
by those who love a job well done.

Those who took up the legacy of his work
wish to pay homage to him through the publication of this book.

Contents

An Introduction to the Monument

The Alhambra was an authentic palatine city, walled-in and independent from the city of Granada. It was built by the Nasrid sultans during the final period of Muslim rule on the Iberian Peninsula.

A Bit of History

The Alhambra (*Qal'at al-Hamra*, red castle) was the bastion of the last Muslim kingdom on the Iberian Peninsula: the Nasrid dynasty of Granada (1238-1492). From this site, the fragile Nasrid monarchy — militarily and economically besieged by the Christian kings, to whom it paid tribute — managed to resist for two and a half centuries while simultaneously attaining its greatest cultural and scientific splendor. Skillful diplomatic policy, natural resources, and the development of both industry and foreign trade were the key factors in the Nasrid dynasty's long existence. Nasrid sultans built the Alhambra and transformed Granada into one of the era's most beautiful and important cities.

Muhammad I ibn Nasr, founder of the Nasrid dynasty, made the wise de-

View of the Alhambra and the Sierra Nevada

cision to abandon the palaces of the bustling, intriguing, and dangerous Alcazaba Cadima (Old) in the Albaicín and transfer his residence to the other side of the Darro River, atop the hill referred to as the "Sabika," a safer and more strategic enclave. To do so, he canalized the water of the river, passing it through the Acequia Real (Royal Canal) toward the dry hill, and restored the old fortress that had been there since the ninth century. The silhouette of the Alhambra began to appear in the Granada landscape. Once the kingdom and its military defense had been established, the monarch builders par excellence of the Alhambra were Yusuf I (1333-1353) and his son Muhammad V (1353-1391); the fourteenth century would become the golden age of the Nasrid kingdom. During the following century, a dark and unstable period began, culminating in the Kingdom of Granada's conquest by the Catholic Monarchs. After ten years of harsh confrontation (1482-1492), on January 2,

The Surrender of Granada*, 1880-1881. Work by Francisco Padilla.*

1492, Boabdil, the last king of the Alhambra, handed over the city keys to the Catholic Monarchs.

The beauty hidden in the palaces of theAlhambra fascinated the conquerors when they took over the city. The Alhambra's premises became the property of the Christian kings, who inhabited them and kept them alive as a symbol of the new power. As a result, it remains the only medieval Arab palace still in existence today.

These monarchs occupied the Alcazaba, the fortresses and the Nasrid Royal House (the Mexuar, the Palace of Comares and the Palace of the Lions). The Alhambra's remaining palaces and residences were distributed among members of their court, granting the Alhambra its own jurisdiction as a city

— independent from that of Granada — and designating the Count of Tendilla as mayor. The Christian residents of this palatine city created a kind of small court that would conserve and inhabit the rest of the houses and palaces, even adopting many Muslim customs. The population was thus constituted by a curious blend of Christians and Moriscos (Muslims who adopted the Catholic religion, often only in appearance,so that they could stay in Spain).

With the arrival of the Bourbons to the Spanish crown, the Alhambra fell from grace. Its inhabitants had supported the Habsburgs during the succession conflict over the Crown of Spain, from 1700 to 1713, which meant that they didn't exactly rouse the sympathy of the new Spanish royal family. When French troops invaded Spain from 1808 to 1812, they occupied the Alhambra and transformed its palaces into barracks. They mined various towers when they withdrew, destroying several, as well as nearly all of the Medina.

As a result of these eighteenth- and nineteenth-century vicissitudes, the Alhambra was left in an unfortunate state of utter neglect. It was found in such conditions by the romantic travelers and artists who reached Granada and fixed it with their poetic, dreaming gaze: staring towards the past, fascinated by the exotic site and its surrounding landscape. These were exceptional witnesses who called for its restoration while spreading the singular image of Granada throughout the world, especially Washington Irving with his *Tales of the Alhambra*.

The Alhambra was declared a National Monument in 1870 and a World Heritage Site in 1984.

A Walled-In Palatine

The Alhambra was an independent palatine city attached to the city of Granada. Its fortified enclosure encompassed a city designed to service the sultans and organized into three sections: the Alcazaba, the palaces and the Medina.

This palatine city — the surface of which measures about ten hectares atop a bare hill, only visible to the outside from the perimeter of connected towers along the wall — was inaccessible to most of the Kingdom of Granada's inhabitants. The fortified defensive towers simultaneously served as housing, storehouses, or gates, and guards stood over the façade of its double rampart where four gates, arranged in L-shapes under the turrets and very

View of Granada and the Sierra Nevada, *1837. Lithograph according to Girault de Prangey.*

closely monitored, gave access to the interior of the mysterious Alhambra. Once inside, other more direct access gates, also guarded, opened onto the different sections of the enclosure.

The Generalife is located beyond the walls of the palatine city: an estate and leisure palace, independent of the Alhambra, used by the Nasrid sultans as a place for rest and retreat.

Of these four gates set into the wall, two were along the western part: the Puerta de la Justicia (Gate of Justice) and the Puerta de las Armas (Gate of Arms), which granted access to the Alcazaba and the palaces. The other two gates were located along the eastern part: the Puerta de los Siete Suelos (Gate of the Seven Floors), which provided access to the Medina, or the people's area, and the Puerta del Arrabal (Gate of the Arrabal), which served as the exit toward the Generalife.

The enclosure consisted of two clearly differentiated sections: the "High Alhambra," in the southeastern area, and the "Low Alhambra," in the northeast, connected by two main streets or arteries: the Real Alta street (Higher Royal Street)[1] and the Real Baja street (Lower Royal Street)[2]. The center contained the Mezquita Mayor (Main Mosque), which, as in all Muslim cities, was the hub around which the rest of the city's activity revolved.

NOTES

[1] The Higher Royal Street began beside the Wine Gate. It ran along the southern side of what is today the Palace of Charles V, along the current Royal Street and along the path that travels the Secano, until reaching the Torre del Cabo de la Carrera (Tower at the End of the Street).

[2] The Lower Royal Street ran parallel to the Higher one. It stemmed from the now-vanished Patio of Comares and passed along the southern façade of the Mexuar and the Palaces of Comares and the Lions, crossing the Partal and continuing up to the Torre de los Picos, or Tower of the Pointed Battlements (Gate of the Arrabal), where it came to an end.

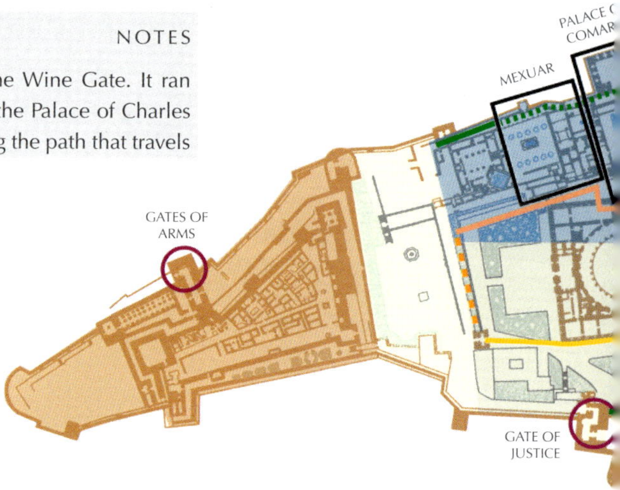

MILITARY AREA, where the garrison responsible for the citadel's safety lived.

RESIDENTIAL AND PALATINE AREA, occupied by the royal family,where official court life took place. In addition to the three palaces that constituted the Nasrid Royal House, there were other palaces and noble houses in this area, which leads us to conclude that the Alhambra's most distinguished families would have lived here.

CIVILIAN AREA, the people's neighborhood, where the majority of the population would have lived: civil servants, domestic attendants, artisans and other residents, all responsible for ensuring the city's necessities and smooth operation. Given the quantity of archaeological remnants found here, we know that the most populous area, today known as the Secano, corresponds to the region with the most intense colors.

Likewise, there were three areas or neighborhoods based on the activity or social contract that characterized the people living there. The area where the people themselves resided was the Medina (city), located in the most densely populated part, which we know today as the Secano, in the High Alhambra. The garrison responsible for the citadel's safety lived in the Alcazaba; this also included the towers and gates located along the walls. The nobility and upper class inhabitants lived in the residential palatine area, which, in addition to the three palaces (Mexuar, Comares, and Lions), occupied part of the Partal area in the Low Alhambra.

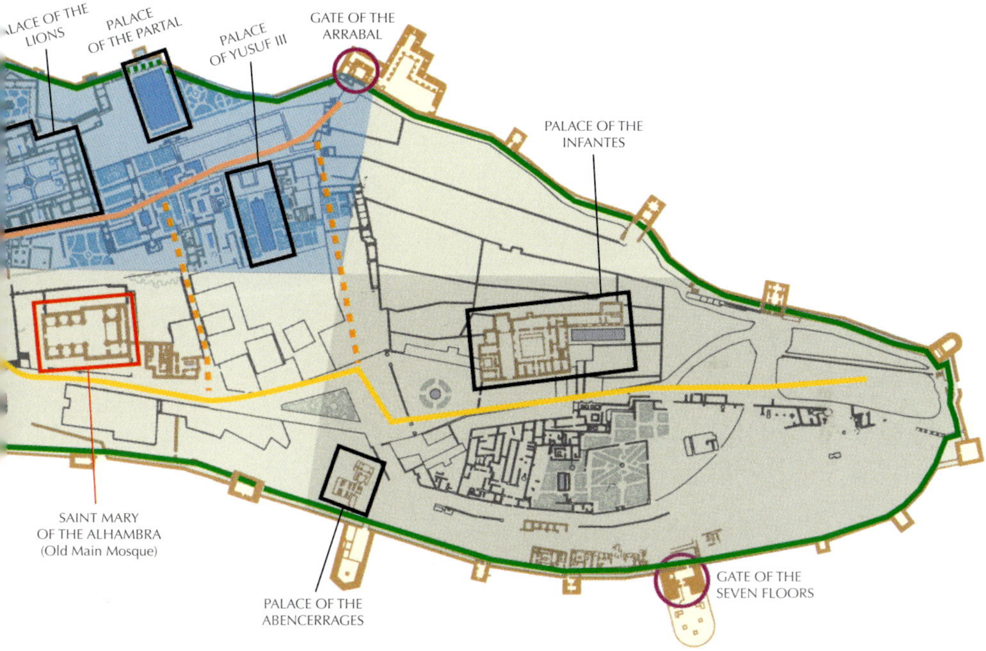

ENCIRCLEMENT ROAD or PATROL PATH. Surrounds the entire enclosure along the inner face of the rampart, running beside or beneath the towers.

LOWER ROYAL STREET. Traversed the palatine zone from end to end. The route of this street is clear and certain along most of its sections; in others, it is an approximate reconstruction.

HIGHER ROYAL STREET. Traversed the entire Medina. It was the longest and surely the most travelled street in the whole Alhambra. As is true of the Lower Royal Street, the route marked is an approximation drawn up from studies and from sections that have been clearly determined. Part of the route coincides with the current Calle Real (Royal Street) of the Alhambra.

SECONDARY ROADS. These are the most difficult to delineate, although we know that they existed and served to connect the Higher and Lower Streets.

Information on Visiting

It is essential to keep in mind that, for conservation reasons, the time of accessfor the area of the Nasrid Palaces is marked on each ticket. You will not be allowed to access them beyond this time, so it is crucial to take note of these circumstances as soon as you acquire the ticket or make an online reservation.

The ticket for a general visit to the Alhambra provides access to all areas open to the public. The route is structured around three primary independent spaces, and you will visit all the rest as you move from one to the other:

- *THE ALCAZABA*. Accessed from the left side, next to the Plaza de los Aljibes (Plaza of the Cisterns). 1
- *THE NASRID PALACES*. The entrance is found next to the northern side of the Palace of Charles V. 2 *Take note of the time indicated on your ticket.*
- *THE GENERALIFE*. May be accessed from various points, depending on when you arrive (before or after visiting the palaces) and on which part of the premises you use to access it:

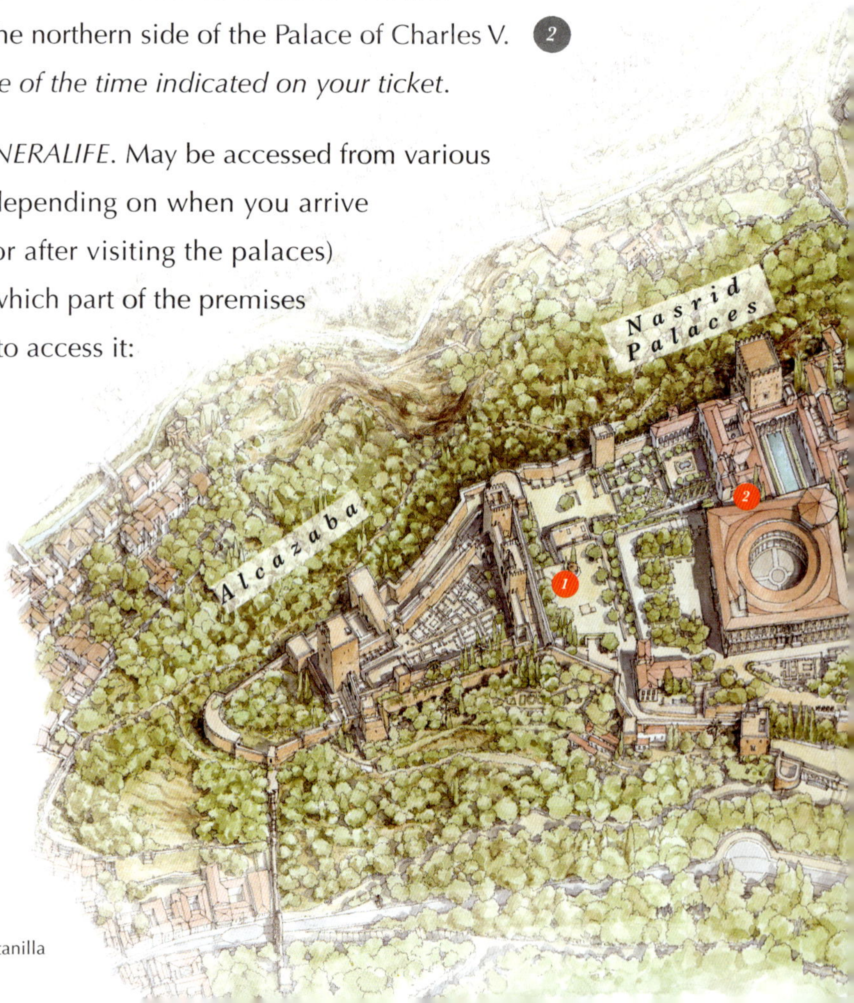

Drawing by Carlos Quintanilla

THE MONUMENT

a. Through the main entrance (entrance pavilion). 3

b. Through the inspection point located beside the Parador de San Francisco, crossing the PATH OF THE SECANO. 4

c. Upon exiting the palaces, walking along the PASEO DEL PARTAL (Partal Promenade) AND THE TOWERS. 5

PATH OF THE SECANO

PARTAL PROMENADE AND THE TOWERS

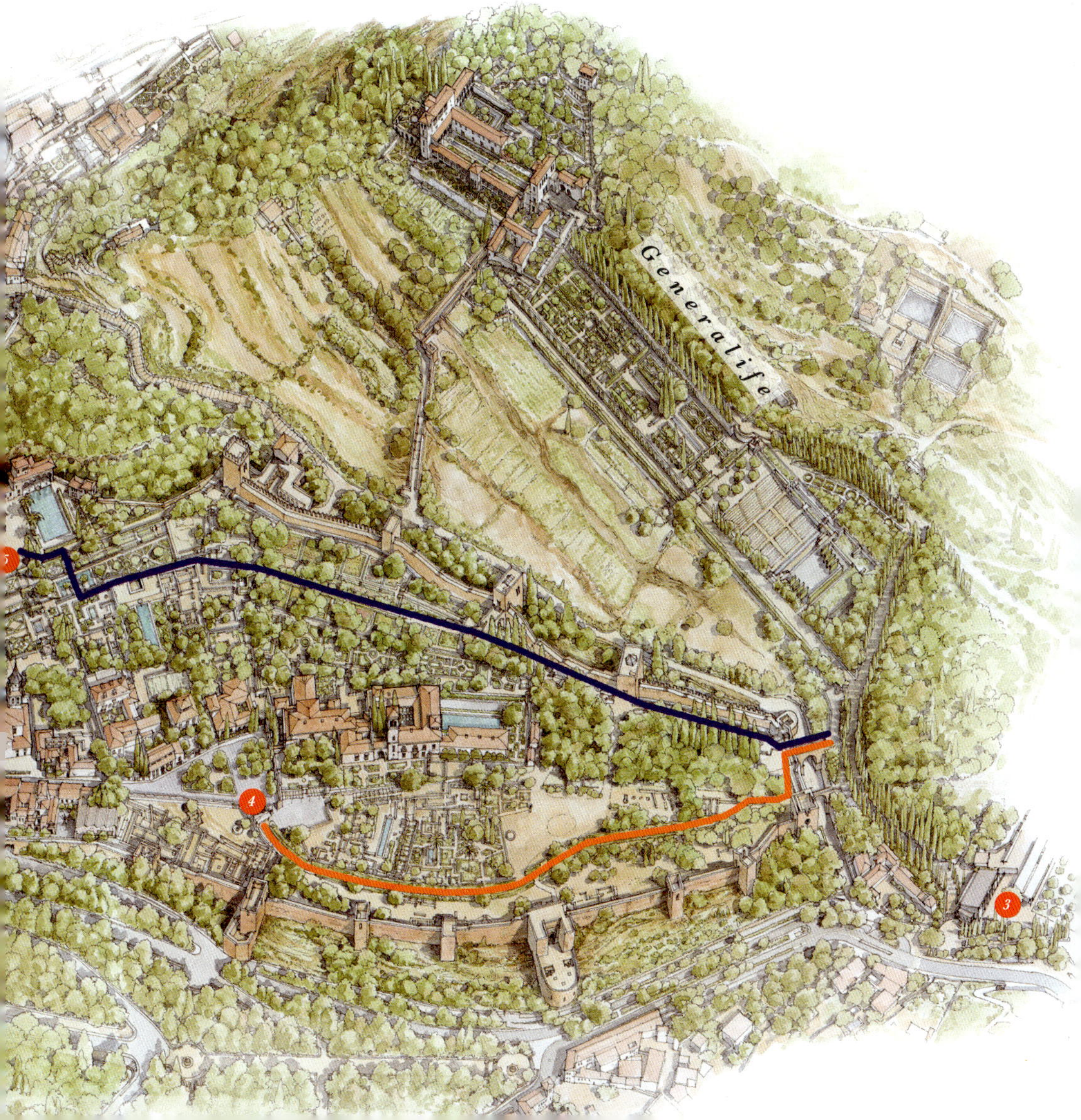

The Muslim Peoples, Masters of al-Ándalus (711-1492)

The Muslims quickly and easily conquered al-Ándalus, as they named the territory of the Iberian Peninsula that we know as Spain today. At the beginning of the eighth century, the Visigoth king who controlled Spain was considerably weakened by the corruption and disputes among his leaders, which meant that the Muslim occupation of his territories, coming from the other side of the Strait, was very swift. The existing Christian and Jewish communities were tolerated in exchange for tribute; in this way, the population of al-Ándalus became a mixture of creeds and ethnicities.

A priori, it could be difficult to understand why the Muslim peoples, who included "holy war" among their fundamental religious precepts, would permit the coexistence of other religions in the areas they occupied. The explanation lies in the fact that Judaism and Christianity were also monotheistic religions, linked to Islam through Abraham (the father of all three religions). Moreover, the Muslims called Jews and Christians *Ahl al-kitab*, which means "people of the book" (the Bible), from which the Muslims, too, assumed some traditions and revelations prior to Allah's message. This is why they granted special status to Jews and Christians.

But if there is one thing that characterized the Muslims' time in al-Ándalus, it was the fragmentation and weakness of its territories; theirs would never be a peaceful domination. These were times of continuous wars, whether with the Christians, who were gradually closing the net from the north, or with the Muslims themselves — including some who were actually from al-Ándalus and others from North African tribes who continually invaded from the south. Such circumstances meant that, in order to keep the peace in the territories, their masters resorted to policies based on pacts and alliances. Domination of al-Ándalus, and consequently of Granada as well, passed through various different periods over the course of eight centuries:

Dependent emirate (711-756)

In the year 711, seven thousand Muslim warriors, mostly Berbers and led by Tariq ibn Ziyab, crossed the Gibraltar Strait and defeated Don Rodrigo (Visigoth king) in the vicinity of Algeciras. This was the first of many more victories that would culminate in a rapid Islamization of the country. In this first period, the conquered territories were ruled by governors who answered directly to the Caliph of Damascus.

Independent emirate (756-929)

This period took shape around the figure of Abd al-Rahman I (of the Umayyad Dynasty), who disembarked in Almuñécar, on the Granadan Coast; became the lord of Sevilla; and, in the vicinity of Córdoba, defeated the emir of al-Ándalus, thus establishing an independent emirate. Abd al-Rahman I governed as an independent sovereign without having to answer to anyone, creating an organized and prosperous state that lasted for nearly two hundred years.

Caliphate (929-1013)

This period began with Abd al-Rahman III, who was declared caliph and prince of the believers and established the Caliphate of Córdoba. Córdoba would achieve its greatest splendor during this era. Meanwhile, Granada would remain in the background, submissive before the Caliphate.

Taifa Kingdoms: the Zirid Kingdom of Granada (1013-1090)

When the Umayyads and the Caliphate of Córdoba collapsed in the early eleventh century, al-Ándalus was left divided into tiny kingdoms or governments called "Taifa Kingdoms," each dominated by a family or dynasty that would frequently fight against the others. The Zirids settled in Granada, a dynasty comprising four kings under whose rule the capital of the territory was shifted — from the vanished city of Elvira to Granada, which would emerge with the Zirids as a kingdom.

The Almoravids and Almohads (1090-1231)

This period could be classified as that of "Berber rule," which brought about greater religious fanaticism and engendered a cultural regression. The Almoravids were Berbers from the desert, recently converted to Islam; departing North Africa, they entered al-Ándalus, which was now severely weakened by the continuous conflicts among the emirs of the Andalusian taifas, and violently defeated the Zirids. The story would soon be repeated: another North African Berber tribe would appear, the Almohads, and would dominate Muslim Spain through the first third of the thirteenth century.

This century marks the Muslim decline in al-Ándalus; their power would be reduced by the powerful efforts of Castile and Aragon.

The Nasrids of the Kingdom of Granada (1238-1492)

This was the last Muslim dynasty to rule in Spain, taking shape around the Nasr or Nasrid family that lived in Arjona. Among its most noteworthy figures was Muhammad (called Ibn Yusuf ibn Nasar ibn al-Ahmar), who was the great opportunist of this era and its disputes and unrest, whose leaders, basically improvised, sought to control the region. Following various victories in a series of territories, al-Ahmar became progressively more popular among the Muslims — a popularity further increased by the gradual losses suffered by his rivals, whose territories the Christians were continuously reconquering.

Al-Ahmar, also known as "the Magnificent," entered Granada in 1238. For chronological purposes, this date is considered the beginning of the Nasrid Kingdom of Granada. This kingdom, the very last of Muslim Spain, encompassed the current complete provinces of Granada, Málaga and Almería, as well as parts of Jaén, Córdoba, Seville and Cádiz.

Muhammad I (al-Ahmar) was declared a vassal of King Fernando III of Castile, which meant that Granada assured his stability and continuation. But Muhammad I will doubtlessly go down in history for having begun construction of the Alhambra.

The Ascent to the Alhambra

Of the various possible access routes into the monument, the best is the one that passes through the Alhambra Woods, due to their monumental and scenic beauty.

Gate of the Pomegranates
Puerta de las Granadas

Gate of the Pomegranates

Fountain of the Tomato, in the Alhambra Woods.

Detail of the
Gate of the Pomegranates

Among the Alhambra's possible access routes, the ascent from the Plaza Nueva (New Plaza) over the Cuesta de Gomérez (the Gomérez Slope) is, for its scenic and historical value, the most emblematic. After climbing the slope, the Gate of Pomegranates appears before us, majestic and triumphant. The emperor Charles V had it built into the rampart that linked the Alcazaba to the Torres Bermejas (Auburn Towers) on the Mauror mountain, replacing an ancient Arab gate. Constructed in 1536 by Pedro Machucha according to the Renaissance standards of style, the symbol of the city, in addition to the dressed stone and the main façade's imperial shield, stands out: the three large pomegranates that provide the finishing touches and establish its name.

ALHAMBRA WOODS   BOSQUE DE LA ALHAMBRA

Gate of the Bib-Rambla (or Gate of the River) in the Alhambra Woods. It was brought here from its original enclave in the city.

Alhambra Woods

Passing through the gate, the dense, hundred-year-old Alhambra Woods welcome the visitor and draws him through its paths in an aura of mystery. This forest didn't exist in the medieval area because of the citadel's military nature; it later took shape with more varied species: elms, horse chestnuts, lime trees, maples, and so forth. In the "cumulous surge of the paths' deep greenness on the Alhambra slope" [Juan Ramón Jiménez], the water runs and murmurs through jets and crevices.

It is recommended that you ascend either along the left slope (steeper and more direct) or along the central path. The former contains a monument to Washington Irving. Scattered along the central path are the Puerta de Bib-Rambla (the Bib-Rambla Gate, or Gate of the River), the Fuente del Tomate (Fountain of the Tomato), and the monument to Ángel Ganivet, Granada-born intellectual from the Generation of '98. From this point, following the route that branches off to the left and guided by the murmur of the water, you will reach the esplanade of the Gate of the Justice and the Pillar of Charles V.

Canal of the Alhambra

Pillar of Charles V

Pillar of Charles V
Pilar de Carlos V

Ornamental detail of the pillar

Among the jewels of the Granadan Renaissance, this pillar was designed by Pedro Machuca and built by Nicolao de Corte in 1545. The water flows from three figureheads representing the three rivers of Granada: the Darro, the Genil, and the Beiro. Above them, we find a console in Latin that alludes to Emperor Charles V; the imperial coat of arms is on the upper part. The pillar also displays other decorative motifs, like children tossing water with snails and mythological scenes.

Gate of Justice
Puerta de la Justicia

Dubbed al-Sharia by the Nasrids, this gate has been, since 1348 in the times of Yusuf I, the most important and magnificent entrance to the Alhambra's walled enclosure. The entrance consists of two wide horseshoe arches; its keystones contain, respectively, a hand and a key, Islamic symbols that represent the five precepts of the Koran and the key to Paradise. Over the second arch, above the Arabic inscription dedicated to the gate's founder, the Catholic Monarchs placed an image of the Virgin with the Child, a German Gothic-style piece from the fifteenth century, as a symbolic expression of the new Christian rule. This is a copy; the original figure is found in Granada's Museo de Bellas Artes (Museum of Fine Arts).

The defensive nature of this tower-gate is apparent in the large opening between its arches, designed for launching projectiles toward attackers, and in the L-shaped entrance with seats for the guards. The rear façade is modest, with a horseshoe arch and some interesting remnants of adorned ceramic.

Wine Gate Puerta del Vino

It is believed that the name originates from the time when wine was deposited here for consumption by the Alhambra's inhabitants (as of 1556). However, this gate, originally named Bib al-hamra (red) may have later been confused with al-jamra (wine). It has a direct entrance, without a defensive bend, and allows access to the Higher Royal Street, the heart of the Medina. The Medina was kept closed off and isolated from the sultans' palaces and from the fortress. The pointed horseshoe arches stand out in the gate's double façade, as do the double windows on the top floor. There is a marked contrast between the ornamentation of these windows; the one overlooking the Plaza of the Cisterns is older and more austere.

Wine Gate

Gate of Justice

The Alcazaba

was the very first of all the structures built in the Alhambra. The others were constructed in the shelter of the citadel and the ramparts.

The Alcazaba is the oldest part of the Alhambra, built atop the remnants of an ancient castle; the site's other structure will gradually emerge around its shelter and that of the rampart. When al-Ahamar acceded to the throne of Granada in 1238, he decided to leave the Albaicín, where Granada's kings had lived until then, in the Alcazaba Cadima (Old Alcazaba). He chose, as the place to establish his residence, the opposite hill, the "Sabika," beyond the city of Granada, separated from it by the valley of the Darro River — but from which the city could be controlled. Indeed, the city and its inhabitants felt very close by.

The area was used for military purposes; the entire palatine city of the Alhambra was defended from the Alcazaba. In a triangular way, the central area contained the military quarter, where officers and some of the guards resided. It is closed off by a double rampart punctuated with towers sketching the uneven line of the fortress and it conceals a

The Alcazaba viewed from the Albaicín

trench or patrol path among its wall-walks[1].

Over time, the Alcazaba has been gradually transformed by the interventions of its different denizens. In its primitive core, delimited by the most interior wall, the Alhambra began to hum. Little by little, its defensive power improved: strategically located towers were erected among various superimposed ramparts and a patrol path. The Christians also left their mark, building bastions[2] — and even gardens when the fortress no longer had anything else to defend.

NOTES

[1] Defense paths, or *adarves*: paths located on top of a rampart, behind the battlements.

[2] The Granadan Muslims had never outfitted the Alhambra for the advances engendered by the most modern artillery machines. Post-conquest, the Christians were the ones who performed a series of alterations — in the Alcazaba and in some of the ramparts' towers — by building bastions. A bastion is a fortified stronghold projected toward the exterior of the fortress's main section, generally at the corners. It was used to more effectively resist the artillery damage inflicted by enemy troops; it also served as a platform on which to position their own artillery.

Tower of Homage and the "Broken" Tower.
The double rampart and the trench are also visible.

The patrol path along
the northeastern section

The Alcazaba trench.
In the background,
the Tower of the Vela.

The Citadel

Drawing by Carlos Quintanilla

1. *"Broken" Tower*
2. *Tower of Homage*
3. *Tower of the Cubo*
4. *Military District*
5. *Gate of Arms*
6. *Tower of the Vela*
7. *Tower of the Hidalgos*
8. *Bastion of the Darro*
9. *Tower of the Pólvora*
10. *Tower of the Sultan*
11. *Garden of the Defense-Paths*
12. *Adarguero Tower*

3
2
1
Entrance
4
12
11

THE ALCAZABA'S

Seen from the Alhambra, the Albaicín is like a hurricane of beauty, a sweet threat that pursues and astonishes.

[RAFAEL GUILLÉN. *Granada, invención del aire* (*Granada, an air invention*).]

From the different towers scattered along its course, the Alcazaba Granada's first lookout today. Here, the landscape is the authentic protagonist accompanying our steps... The Albaicín, where villas with gardens, churches, and a multitude of roofs combine architecture and greenery with surprising harmony...

LANDSCAPE

The Albaicín viewed from the Alcazaba

The lower city, where modern buildings coexist with churches and noble palaces, built after the conquest as a symbol of the new victorious culture...

Sierra Nevada and the meadows of Granada that change their color and their view with every season of the year, with every hour of the day...

MILITARY DISTRICT BARRIO CASTRENSE

This was the residential area for the sultan's elite guard and some of the soldiers responsible for defending the Alhambra; it is found in the heart of the Alcazaba, surrounded by wall-walks and towers. Distributed on both sides of what would have been a central road, the remnants of dwellings,

The Military District and the towers along the eastern section (Tower of Homage and the "Broken" Tower)

workshops, silos, storehouses, ovens and dungeons are still preserved, as well as the baths and the water cistern that supplied them. Among these ruins, we can appreciate the typical layout of a Muslim home: entrance, small courtyard, rooms ringing the courtyard, and latrine.

The Tower of Homage from the Military District. Below, the same tower with the Generalife in the background.

Tower of Homage
Torre del Homenaje

It is very common to find a keep in all medieval castles; the fortress chief generally lived here. From a strategic point of view, this tower tended to be the last refuge within a fortification and the most defensible space, maintaining certain autonomy within the castle. With six floors, from which the city and surrounding territory was controlled, this is the Alhambra's tallest tower. Concealed within its walls, on the top floor, is a small dwelling with four rooms and an inner courtyard — which, it is thought, may have housed Al-Hamar, the first Nasrid sultan, at certain points. Archaeological studies deduce that the keep may have been built atop the remnants of another much older tower, dating from the ninth century.

In the lower part of this tower, on the northeast vertex, separated from it by the patrol path, the Christians erected the TORRE DEL CUBO (TOWER OF THE CUBO), a sixteenth-century bastion that was built over the ancient Muslim tower called the Tahona, which remained hidden inside. Almost all of the Alhambra's bastions, like this one, are Christian defensive reinforcements.

The Tower of the Cubo from inside the trench

Gate of Arms   Puerta de las Armas

This tower, dating from the late thirteenth century, is one of the four exterior gates inserted into the rampart that runs along the entire perimeter of the Alhambra. In the Nasrid era, it must have been the most important, as it was the most direct access point between the Alhambra and the city of Granada. Subjects entered the citadel and the palaces through this gate in order to resolve their bureaucratic affairs and be attended by the sultan or his government staff. Before entering, however, they had to lay down their arms (hence the name) and cross a stretch of patrol path highly policed by the guards from the wall-walks. Its interior architecture, uneven and L-shaped, clearly declares its defensive function and military nature. But this gate, being the primary entryway to the Alhambra, also fulfilled a civic task: the

Gate of Arms. The subjects of the Albaicín typically accessed the citadel through this gate.

distribution of transit in two directions. For this reason, the other side offers two exits: one toward the citadel and another toward the medina and the palaces. This civic function, as well as providing greater human circulation, explains why this gate (as opposed to other edifices with a strictly military use) is more heavily ornamented; this is noticeable both in the decorations on the horseshoe arch of the exterior façade and in the interior vaults, which are divided into three sections. The vaults in the first and third section are formed with curved segments and are painted to imitate brick.

The tower rises above the ramparts' façade to avoid danger and harass intruders. From the terrace, the Alhambra's defensive system is clearly visible (the double rampart, trench or patrol path, and towers).

Detail of the vault of curved segments covering the Gate of Arms

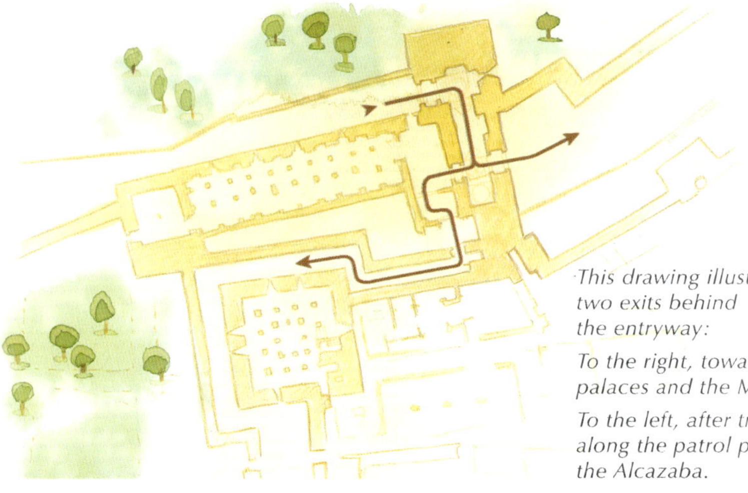

This drawing illustrates the two exits behind the entryway:

To the right, toward the palaces and the Medina.

To the left, after traveling along the patrol path, toward the Alcazaba.

Drawing by Ana Campos

Interior of the Gate of Arms

Tower of the Vela from the Bastion of the Darro

[3] There is a curious tradition in connection with the bell in the Tower of the Vela and January 2nd. Every year on this day, many single Granadan woman climb up to the terrace of the tower and ring the bell in hopes of finding a husband.

[4] The ravelin is a triangular building facing the body of the main edifice, generally on the other side of the trench, which was designed to keep back the attacking forces and protect the curtain walls.

Tower of the Vela
Torre de la Vela

This tower, referred to as the Torre Mayor (Main Tower) in the Nasrid era, is the privileged watchtower over the hollow of Granada, as well as the most emblematic one for Granada natives. The panorama fans outward toward the majestic Sierra Nevada peaks and toward the Vega, where the urban groupings inexorably advance. It has four floors distributed among dwellings, storehouses, and a basement with a dungeon. Like nearly all of the Alhambra's towers, it was crowned with battlements in Nasrid times. From this enclave, through a system of towers and fortresses scattered across strategic locations, the Kingdom of Granada's vast territory was surveyed and controlled. In this tower, as the tradition goes, the standards of the Catholic Monarchs were raised when they entered the Alhambra so that all the city's inhabitants could see them. The bell was put in place following the conquest. Since then, its sound in the belfry has marked the rhythms of the city and the irrigation of the meadows. It still rings on special occasions and on the January 2 holiday[3], a memorial day for the city's capture by the Catholic Monarchs.

This tower's terrace is the best place to appreciate the REVELLÍN[4] (RAVELIN), also called the BALUARTE DE LA MEZQUITA DE SOBRE DARRO (BASTION OF THE MOSQUE OVER THE DARRO), the largest bastion in the entire Alhambra, which the Catholic Monarchs commissioned on westernmost side of the Alcazaba — and which, viewed within the fortress as a whole, resembles the prow of a ship.

Garden of the Defense-Paths and Tower of the Sultana

Garden of the Defense-Paths
Jardín de los Adarves

Give alms, woman, as there is nothing in the world
like the shame of being blind in Granada.

[FRANCISCO DE ICAZA]

This is the area that has undergone the greatest transformations over the years. After conquest, like other parts of the Alcazaba, alterations were made to this southern flank in order to improve defenses. Its trench was filled with soil with the idea of building an artillery platform and a new, more modern rampart was erected. Later, gardens were created here, coinciding with the end of the war against the Moriscos, who had revolted and who, as losers, were definitively expelled in the first years of the seventeenth century. It became one of the most beautiful places in the Alhambra. A crude, austere military space has become an enchanted space: an open window to the mountains, the woods, the peak of Mauror, and the Auburn Towers.

Tower of the Pólvora in the Garden of the Defense-Paths. In the background, the Auburn Towers.

The Catholic Monarchs, Architects of the Unity of the Spanish Kingdoms

Before Isabel and Fernando secured the throne, the Spanish territory was divided into four independent kingdoms: Castile, Aragon, Navarra and Granada. Together, the kingdoms of the Crown of Castile and the Crown of Aragon occupied nearly seventy percent of the territory. The Kingdom of Navarra was the smallest and least populous of the lot; the Kingdom of Granada, the last territory on the Peninsula that remained under Muslim rule, was the most coveted. Isabel and Fernando achieved not only the unity of Spain under a single ruling monarchy, but also — sometimes by virtue of their diplomatic and marital policies (they married their children with heirs to the throne of the primary European royal families) and sometimes by virtue of military victories — extended their dominion beyond Spanish borders.

Two events marked the lives and political activity of these monarchs and were decisive in securing the unity of Spain's kingdoms and its birth as a modern state: *their marriage and the conquest of the Kingdom of Granada.*

Isabel and Fernando's marriage and the union of their respective Crowns (Castile and Aragon)

Before 1469, the year they were married, Isabel and Fernando had to overcome an endless series of difficulties. First of all, they were second cousins, which meant that they needed a papal bull to be married. Further, Isabel had several suitors vying for her hand — all far more important men than Fernando as far as the Castilian nobility was concerned: King Alfonso of Portugal, the Duke of Guyenne (brother of the King of France), and the Duke of Gloucester (brother of the King of England), as well as several other Spaniards. To make matters worse, Fernando was unpopular among the Castilian nobles after being vetoed by Isabel's brother, Enrique IV, "the Impotent," King of Castile, and by the all-powerful Marquis of Villena.

What to do in the face of such enormous problems? Fernando did have the support of his father, Juan II of Aragon, and his maternal grandfather, Don Fadrique Enríquez, admiral of Castile. Besides, he brought to his aid the fearsome archbishop of Toledo, Don Alonso Carrillo, who would ultimately serve as the architect of his wedding. For the time being, Juan II of Aragon, in order to increase his son's value for Isabel and the Castilian nobles, named him King of Sicily, the title with which he would be married.

So great was the opposition to Fernando that the villainous Marquis of Villena even tried kidnapping Isabel in hopes of marrying her to Alfonso V of Portugal. At the same time, he tried to obstruct Fernando's arrival at Castile, where he was set to meet Isabel, as it seemed that they had already agreed upon a possible marriage. On reaching Castile, Fernando ingeniously disguised himself as a mule driver,accompanied by an entourage of just four friends. Thus, the two young people were at last able to meet, and they were engaged to marry.

The problem of their kinship still needed to be resolved. The archbishop Alonso Carrillo issued a false papal bull, allowing them to marry in 1469. The genuine bull was granted by Pope Sixtus IV in 1471, two years later.

The Conquest of the Nasrid Kingdom of Granada

Despite the hectic life they lived and how constantly busy it kept them, Isabel and Fernando's thoughts never strayed from Granada. It served as an excuse to start the war against the King of Granada, Abu l-Hasan Ali — who had refused to pay the 150,000 maravedís that were stipulated as tribute and who had himself initiated the hostilities — taking the city of Zahara (Cádiz) by surprise in 1481. The astute Catholic Monarchs also knew how to take advantage of the power struggles and intrigues afflicting the Granadan court at the time, centering on King Abu l-Hasan Ali, his son (Boabdil), and his brother (El Zagal).

They launched an initial offensive in response to Abu l-Hasan Ali's affront, taking the important city of Alhama in 1482, on the border of the Granadan kingdom. In the Battle of Lucena, they took Boabdil prisoner and, although they would later free him, his liberty would be granted in exchange for his becoming a vassal of Castile. Little by little, the kingdom's most important cities would fall into Fernando and Isabel's hands: Ronda in 1485, Loja in 1486, Vélez-Málaga and Málaga in 1487. Between 1488 and 1489, Huéscar, Vélez Blanco, Vélez Rubio, Baza, Guadix and Almería would follow.

In the aftermath of these conquests, Granada was left almost completely isolated; in 1491, the Catholic Monarchs asked Boabdil, who held the throne at the time, to hand over the city. When the Moorish king refused, the Christians launched a siege. They set up their encampment in the Vega de Granada, in a place they called Santa Fe. It was there that they signed the Capitulations with Christopher Columbus — according to which the Monarchs would finance his voyage to the New World, establishing, in exchange, the boundaries of Castile beyond the seas.

In the face of the siege and chokehold he was subjected to, Boabdil finally handed over the keys to the city on January 2, 1492.

Isabel I of Castile and Fernando II of Aragon had managed to extend their sovereign power to nearly all of the Spanish Kingdoms; only Navarra remained, which was annexed in 1512. With the conquest of the Kingdom of Granada, they fulfilled their greatest wish — and it is perhaps for this reason that their bodies eternally rest in this city.

The Medina

was the most densely populated space in the entire Alhambra, an authentic neighborhood of the people, where most of the precincts' houses and buildings were found.

The Medina

Drawing by Carlos Quintanilla

1. ***Church of Saint Mary of the Alhambra***
   (built on the plot of the ancient Main Mosque)
2. ***Baths of the Mosque***
3. ***Royal Street of the Alhambra***
   (its route coincides with part of the ancient Higher Royal Road)
4. ***Remnants of the Palace of the Abencerrages***
5. ***Remnants of Nasrid houses***
6. ***Path of the Secano***
   (follows the same route as the vanished Higher Royal Road)
7. ***Parador San Francisco***
   (former Franciscan convent built a top the remnants of a thirteenth-century Nasrid palace)
8. ***Gate of the Seven Floors***
   (this was the entry way to the Medina from the outside)
9. ***Water Tower***

7
9
5
6
8

Gate of Wine. Marked the entrance to the Higher Royal Street from within the Alhambra.

This was the most populated space in the entire Alhambra, an authentic neighborhood of the people, where most of the precincts' houses and buildings were found.

Since its origins in the era of Al-Hamar (thirteenth century) and until the Christian conquest (fifteenth century), the Alhambra continued to grow within the perimeter of its ramparts until it became an authentic palatine city at the service of the Nasrid nobility and the sultans who occupied its palaces.

It was traversed by two main streets: the Lower Royal Street, which ran through the palace area, and the Higher Royal Street, which ran through the area inhabited by most of the population: civil servants, attendants, craftsmen, and other residents, all responsible for ensuring the city's smooth operation.

Royal Street of the Alhambra. Follows the same route as the ancient Higher Royal Street.

There was also a series of secondary streets that connected to these two primary roads.

This entire urban space, traversed by the Higher Royal Street, was the Medina: a mixture of small dwellings, workshops, and administrative buildings with some large houses and noble palaces. Inside, in the most elevated area toward the southeast, there was a more populated part, the Medina Alta (High Medina), corresponding to the space currently known as the Secano ("dry land"). It acquired this name because it has been the most damaged space in all of the Alhambra (archaeological remains and ruins have reached us from this area alone), due, above all, to the destruction caused here by the Napoleonic troops, who blew it up before making their retreat in the early nineteenth century.

Church of Saint Mary of the Alhambra, built on the same plot as the ancient Mosque.

Pool in what must have been one of the Medina's most important houses

Gate of the Seven Floors. This was the access gate to the Higher Royal Street from outside the Alhambra.

A devastated place in which almost nothing remains of what once had been.

Remnants of the Palace of the Abencerrages

The Secano is traversed by a garden-filled walkway, which was designed by the conservative architect of the Torres Balbás monument in the first third of the twentieth century — based on the route that, it was thought, the ruined part of the Higher Royal Street would have followed in its day. Today, this road is one of the possible connections between the Alhambra and the Generalife. From the path, some of these archaeological remains are visible, as are some of the towers that outlined the rampart. Here, too, is the Gate of the Seven Floors, one of the enclosure's four large gates, through which the Medina was accessed from the outside; it was blown up by the French when they withdrew and had to be redone according to ancient drawings and etchings. It is a place full of mystery: underground, according to the "The Legend of the Moor's Legacy"[1] in *Tales of the Alhambra*, a great

NOTES

[1] "The Legend of the Moor's Legacy":

This legend tells the story of a humble, honest water carrier who would go with his donkey every day to collect fresh water from the Alhambra's wells and then bring it back down to Granada. Such was his kindness that, one night, he helped an old Moor — tired, nearly dying, and asking for help — onto his donkey and took the man into his home. The Muslim told him that if he died, the water carrier must keep a mysterious box he carried with him. The box contained a piece of a candle and an old parchment in Arabic. The water carrier sought the help of a clever Moorish merchant, who translated the parchment for him. After various difficulties, the honest "partners" — with the help of the parchment and the candle — found an extraordinary treasure hidden in one of the seven underground floors that, according to legend, were accessed through this gate.

The Water Tower, beside the aqueduct that carried water from the Generalife to the Alhambra.

treasure was hidden. At the end of the walkway, to the east, is the aqueduct through which the Royal Canal flowed and entered the Alhambra, next to the Water Tower.

Unfortunately, what was once the most bustling and populous neighborhood in the Alhambra has practically disappeared. Only some vestiges of its buildings and urban network remain: the Saint Mary of the Alhambra church (where the old mosque had been), the baths, some houses and palaces (like the current Parador de San Francisco and the remnants of the Palacio de los Abencerrajes, or Palace of the Abencerrages), what's left of the Higher Royal Street... But we can go in and imagine its teeming daily life while we walk down its main road alongside the protagonists of the novel *La Fórmula*[2].

[2] *La Fórmula*:

"We walked hand in hand [...] Along this street, which is called the Higher or Greater Royal street, a group of weavers shouted as they transported, on the backs of beasts, a load of skeins of green- and indigo-dyed wool; we stepped aside to let a squadron of infantry soldiers pass, richly sculpted with linen garments of an immaculate white [...] we stared curiously at both sides of the street, open from west to east: great palaces, protected by walls painted white, pink, or russet, coexist here amid the masses of buildings and houses of lesser ostentation, with workshops open to the street where a group of craftsman readied themselves for their labors. We also passed youths and schoolchildren who carried their tablets and notebooks under their arms or atop their heads [...] Water from a canal enters through an aqueduct beside a tower protected by archers [...] We stopped for a moment, dazzled by the rays of the sun, our breathing labored from the walk: the call of the muezzin so surprised us that we startled abruptly, feeling his cry — "La Ghalib illa Allahhhh...!" — like sparks falling onto our miserable lives." [GARCÍA FRESNEDA, A. Excerpt from *La Fórmula*. Ediciones Miguel Sánchez].

Tower of the Witches and Tower of the Captain, on the southeast rampart, beside the Secano.

THE PALACES
Introduction

These palaces comprise the Royal House or Alcázar, where the Nasrid sultans' domestic and official life took place. They consist of three palaces built in different periods, which are configured into a single court space. After conquest, various rooms were built and integrated into the palace for habitation by the Emperor Charles V.

The palatine space of the Alhambra consists of three Nasrid palace-houses: Mexuar, Comares, and Leones. They were built in different periods by the sultans in power at each point, constituting a single court space, the Casa del Sultán (Sultan's House), where, distributed throughout various spaces, private and family life, official court life, and the management of the kingdom's bureaucratic and administrative matters were developed. They also comprise what is known today as the Casa Real Cristiana (Royal Christian House), a series of rooms and courtyards that Emperor Charles V com-

View of the palaces from the Albaicín

missioned for his own occupation during his visits to Granada — while the grand palace he had planned, also in the Alhambra was being finished.

These were not the only palaces in the Alhambra. Indeed, others were built at different times and in other places, inhabited by sultans or by some of the Alhambra's noblest families: the Palace of the Partal, the Palace of the Abencerrages, the Palace of Yusuf III, and the Palace of the Infantes (currently the Parador de San Francisco).

The entrance to these palaces is found, nearly hidden, beside the north

side of the Palace of Charles V. From the outside, nothing suggests the importance of the precincts; like all Muslim houses, everything significant lies in the interior, concealing its riches from unfamiliar eyes. There is no external display that could manifest the fortunate status of its denizens and disrupt the equality among believers before the Supreme God. These structures were not made with the intention of lasting for posterity; they were built with shoddy materials (clay, wood, and plaster), and their fragility symbolizes the temporary character of life, power, and fortune, as only God is eternal. For this reason, the edifices were continually transformed by successive sultans, who demolished, modified, or annexed new spaces onto the preexisting ones.

It is important to understand that the Muslim peoples had a multifunctional conception of space. As opposed to Western culture, in which each room had a distinct functionality, rooms in Muslim dwellings fulfilled various purposes throughout the day: sitting room, dining room, bedroom... Grasping this makes it much easier to understand our visit to these royal spaces.

One of the gates along the Court of the Myrtles

Column of the Court of the Lions

The Palaces

Drawing by Carlos Quintanilla

1. ***Mexuar***
2. ***Palace of Comares***
3. ***Palace of the Lions***
4. ***Christian Rooms***
5. ***Royal Baths***

Palace and Gardens
of the Partal
4
5
3
Palace
Charles V

The Hispanic-Muslim Home and Domestic Life

Palace of Dar-al-Horra (Albaicín)

If anything determines a people's way of life including their vital space, their houses, and the home they live in with their families, it is their culture, their origins as a social group, their customs or their religion. All these factors have determined a series of specific traits of Muslim homes that are very different from what these would have been like in western Judeo-Christian society.

The first noteworthy and differentiating trait of a Muslim home is the nakedness of its walls, which are lacking windows or ornaments that could be seen from the street to avoid provide any clues regarding who lives there. Unlike in Western culture, where the outside of homes provided clues regarding the illustrious condition of its owners, the Muslim home did not show the greater or lesser status of the persons living there. In neighbourhoods, even the maximum height of the homes was planned so that none of the homes could be visually observed from any of the other homes. If any windows were available, they were located in the top floors and they were very small. The only opening to the exterior was the entrance door, which never provided direct access to the home. The entrance was always constructed at a bend or entering into a hallway that was used as a lobby, where a second door was located, which provided direct access to the home; there was never a straight line from this second door to the first, it was always located to one side so that no one located on the street could see inside the home.

Once inside, the most common feature of all homes was the patio, which provided light and ventilation, and from where the most illustrious rooms of the house could be entered. This patio, larger or smaller depending on the category of the home, usually had a sink or water tank located at its centre. This method of distributing the rooms surrounding a patio was an influence from roman style homes, from which culture Muslims had adopted many features. Some homes even had two patios. In noble homes and palaces, normally the patio also had one or two gantries at its smaller sides. If the size of the patios allowed, they usually included gardens with aromatic plants, lemon trees, orange trees and some vine. This was the central element of the home, from where all spaces were distributed and was the centre of daily life. Not all patios included pools. The sole purpose of the patios of small homes such as those of the Castrense neighbourhood of La Alcazaba, was to provide light and ventilation.

As stated by Professor Antonio Orihuela in his study regarding *Nasrid Homes and Palaces of the XII-XIV centuries*, "having a good patio was probably the main ambition of all citizens of the Nasrid Emirate". It allowed its habitants to be outdoors and enjoy the aroma of the plants and the sound of the water, in private and out of the view of strangers. It also served a representative function since it was the place where guests and visitors were received. Since women could not be seen by any strange male entering the home, because it was prohibited by the religious mandate of "hiyab" (keep women out of sight), the rooms adjacent to the patio were occupied by the master and men in the family. Women occupied the rooms that were located in the top floor and if no top floor was available, then they occupied the rooms located farthest from the patio. In large homes with two patios, the main patio was used for receiving guests and was occupied only by the men and the second patio was used by the women and children. When there were no people present other than family members, women could then move freely about the home, taking care of all the home chores and the education of the children.

Regarding the role of women in social and family life in Islam, not all the women remained hidden. Maids and slaves tended to guests with their

Grijales Street (Albaicín). Clearly represents the urban typology of a Muslim neighborhood: narrow streets with exposed walls, hiding any sign of what might help us imagine what lies behind them.

Saint Gregory Street (Albaicín). The gates were the only element open to the outside along the walls lining any street in Muslim-era Granada.

faces uncovered and were not subjected to the rules of morality, which had to be complied with by free women. The society was patriarchal, the head of the family had absolute power. Prior to marriage, the woman had the right to a dowry and a percentage of their husband's inheritance. Although their religion allowed for a single man to have more than one wife, as many as four, the man was required to prove that he could care for them as well as pay their dowry. Therefore polygamy was not possible in poor families. Only men of a certain economic level could afford more than one wife. Even so, in Nasrid Granada, it was not as frequent as in other places for rich men to have more than one wife.

Another peculiarity of Muslim homes was their use of the space for multiple purposes. Unlike western homes, different rooms did not exists for each function; bedroom, living room, dining room, etc. A single room was used for carrying out all these functions depending on the time of day or the needs of the house. These multi-purpose rooms have their origin in the nomad and itinerant lifestyles of these people in other eras, where the "jaima" (tent) was the only habitable space, which could easily be broken down and included light furniture that could be easily transported. For this reason, when these people colonized other places where they settled permanently such as in the case of Al ándalus, they continued maintaining many of their old customs. Because of this multi-purpose, the rooms did not include large and heavy furniture that was difficult to move from one place to another, as would be the case in a Christian home. Muslims decorated their homes using carpets, cloths, pillows, low tables, arches, cupboards, etc., which could all be easily moved from one location of the house to another and this way, a space used for dining or receiving a guest at a certain hour of the day, could be transformed in the evening into a place for resting and sleeping. According to Professor Antonio Orihuela, "the rooms that define Nasrid homes with patio, to be considered complete are: elbow shaped hallway, main room, secondary room, kitchen and toilet". "To accomplish this, an area measuring at least 50 square metres is required". The kitchens are located inside the terraces.

The last great characteristic of Muslim homes is the importance of water and the installations it included. For these people water was a purifying element that was essential for conducting their religious practices. Also, since it was a scarce good in some of its territories of origin, they always found ways to build channels to bring water into their cities and homes. To accomplish this they used systems that were much more advanced than those that existed in Christian cities. Muslims copied the urban channelling system from the Roman civilization. As described by professor Orihuela, "water from rivers or springs was transported to cities via water channels, which were uncovered during their trajectory until they reached the outside of the city walls. When the water entered the city, it was routed through a series of pipes until reaching the public catchments as well as private ones located inside homes that had these catchments built for them". Medieval Nasrid Granada included a complete water supply network that "allowed citizens, whose homes did not include a water supply, to conveniently have water available just a few metres from their homes". The homes also had latrines and systems used to evacuate waste water. The latrine was located as close as possible to the exterior. These were accessed from the patio so that they would be well ventilated and a room of the house was used specifically for this function, which was isolated from the rest by means of an elbow shaped entrance or a door.

All these elements of Muslim homes and more specifically, that of Nasrid homes in Medieval Granada, also existed in each one of the homes and palaces of the Alhambra; however, in the case of the Alhambra, these elements were available but at a greater scale.

Court of the House of Zafra (Albaicín), possessing all characteristic elements of a Nasrid-era Granadan house.

THE PALACES
The Mexuar

was largely built by Ismail I (1314-1325). It is the oldest of the three and had, at least during a significant period of its history, the greatest public role.

This part of the palaces, at least for much of their history, had a distinct public purpose: administration of justice, Council meetings, and bureaucratic tasks. It is the oldest palace of the three. Largely built by Ismail I (1314-1325), this one has undergone the greatest number of modifications

Exterior of the Palace of the Mexuar. In the foreground, the Court of Machuca.

and refurbishments over time, first by various Nasrid sultans and later by the Christian kings. It has also suffered the greatest damage, particularly in its westernmost area, where the two courts are found; for the most part, only archeological remnants are left. The rest of the palace has been better preserved.

Map of the Mexuar

Drawing by Ana Campos

1. *Court of the Mosque*
2. *Court of Machuca*
3. *Hall of the Mexuar*
4. *Oratory*
5. *Court of the Mexuar:*
   5a. Golden Room
   5b. Façade of the Palace of Comares

Courts of the Mosque

Patios de la Mezquita y de Machuca

This is the first of the patios; only archeological ruins remain. Different hypotheses exist with respect to the edifices that surround it and the function they performed: the most widespread theory is that they were rooms occupied by civil servants responsible for bureaucratic and administrative tasks. Its name is taken from the "Old" Mosque, a small oratory; evidence of its remnants are found in one of its vertices, attributed to Ismail I.

The Court of Machuca is adjacent to the Court of the Mosque, but better conserved. It presents a gallery of arches over the length of the rampart, to which a tower is connected, the Machuca Tower (previously called the

AND OF MACHUCA

Corner of the Court of Machuca

Archeological remnants of the Court of the Mosque

Torre de los Puñales, or the Tower of the Daggers). The tower owes its current name, as does the court, to the fact that Pedro Machuca, architect of the Palace of Charles V, lived in it and in the garden spaces. On the opposite side, presently occupied by a line of dense cypress trees trimmed into arches, there must have been another gallery that provided access to the palace. A small geometrically shaped fountain and a row of orange trees adorn this beautiful garden, which, although different from the original medieval-era court, maintains the magic and charm exuded by the entire Alhambra.

Hall of the Mexuar Sala del Mexuar

This is the first of the palatine spaces that will inspire any visitor's admiration. A project undertaken by sultan Ismail I (1314-1325), it has undergone many alterations over the years. The most significant changes in the Nasrid era were carried out by Yusuf I and Muhammad V; the projects undergone by the Christians post-conquest were the ones that most substantially modified its original configuration. As for its purpose in the medieval period, it

Hall of the Mexuar

actually had many different ones, as is true of most spaces in the Alhambra: the place where the Sura or the Council of Ministers met; where justice was meted out; or, at particular times, as the Hall of the Sultan's Throne. The space was originally smaller and was laid out around four central columns, without the current wooden partition walls. The ceiling was also quite different, opened around an enormous lantern that let out the light and

Hall of the Mexuar

Detail of a tile in the Hall of the Mexuar

was closed off by a high glass dome.

The Christians transformed this space into a chapel (hence the existence of the choir, unthinkable in a Muslim building), and opened the side windows, which hadn't previously existed. They expanded the hall at the back, toward the north side, beneath the choir, and built the upper floor. This changed the appearance not only of the roofs, but also of the entire building. These new building.

Oratory of the Mexuar

These new upper rooms were later inhabited in the modern period by some of the Alhambra's governors. Logically, this diversity of uses and owners over time has also made its mark on the hall's decoration, where the geometric elements of the original Muslim tiles coexist with other Christian elements, like the Pillars of Hercules with the motto *Plus Ultra*, which flanked the old altar of the Christian chapel.

There is an ORATORY at the back, which was not originally adjacent to this hall; its entrance was elsewhere. This is an intimate space with beautiful views of the Albaicín, oriented towards Mecca. Thoroughly restored, its *mihrab* stands out: a niche in the wall where the Koran was placed, adorned by a horseshoe arch and the inscription "...don't be among the careless; come to pray."

Court of the Mexuar
Patio del Mexuar

This court is located at the exit of Mexuar Hall. It has a clear function as a dividing and access area. A small marble basin in the middle dominates the entire space. It has two beautiful sides: to the north, the Pórtico del Cuarto Dorado (Portico of the Golden Room); to the south, the façade of the Palace of Comares.

The GOLDEN ROOM is preceded by a three-arched portico that adorns the court. It owes its name to the golden roof, decorated with gold leaf in the time of the Catholic Monarchs. The Christians made other alterations to the space — like the large window, divided by a Gothic window, as an overlook with seats on either side. As is true of many other places in the Alhambra, the Golden Room displays a combination of Muslim decorative elements with Christian emblems and symbols. Beneath this room is the patrol path, which goes around the entire ramparts. For this reason, we can suppose that nothing built on this north side of the court would have existedat the time of the Palace of the Mexuar's origins, leaving what is now a closed courtyard as an open space that would have faced the outer wall.

The FAÇADE OF THE PALACE OF COMARES delimited access to a more private environment within the palace spaces. It is one of the Alhambra's most important architectural and decorative elements. Mohammad V commissioned it to commemorate the capture of Algeciras

Court of the Mexuar
and façade of the Palace of Comares

Court of the Mexuar and façade of the Golden Room

(1369); as a result of this event, he regained control over the Strait of Gibraltar, which his father had lost in the battle of Salado.

Here, tradition describes the sultan perched at the top of the stairs, in the middle of the impressive façade, seated on his throne, listening to his subjects, meting out justice or receiving foreign ambassadors. Some of the epigraphs inscribed on the façade help us imagine this scene: "My position is that of a crown and my gate is a fork in the road: the West believes that the East is in me..." This is an allegory that clearly refers to the two gates below the phrases. Of the two, only the left-hand gate, after walking along an L-shaped corridor patrolled by guards, led to the large palace courtyard. The

Ceiling of the Golden Room. Its gold leaf finishing is from the Christian era.

Detail of the façade of the Palace of Comares

right-hand door led to rooms possibly designated for servants.

Attractive cedar wood eaves, decorated with plant motifs, crowns the façade. Beneath them, closed windows with wooden latticework make one feel that the space on the other side is no longer public — inhabited only by the sultan and his family, where the eyes of others can no longer gaze.

The Palace of Comares

was built by Yusuf I (1333-1354). As in all great Nasrid houses, the central space is occupied by a court around which the other rooms were organized.

This palace was constructed by Yusuf I (1333-1354), one of the most illustrious Nasrid kings, called "the great emir" for his many political and moral qualities. He was a passionate defender of the sciences and the arts and one of the most vigorous learned figures in the Europe of his time. Decoration was completed by his son Muhammad V (1354-1391). With both, the Nasrid kingdom would attain its greatest splendor.

As one may reasonably imagine, the palace would have a particular use and purpose in its first stage and another different one when it coexisted in time

Court of the Myrtles, north portico.

with the later Palace of the Lions. It belongs to a private residential area within the palaces, although not all of its spaces would take on an exclusively private purpose. Official court functions were also held here, and foreign delegations were received, lending significance to the large size of its central pool and to the majestic Salón del Trono (Throne Room), also known as the Chamber of Ambassadors. It is the very largest room in the entire Alhambra, and, as a result of its symbology and esotericism, was called to witness the grandest events occurring in the Kingdom of Granada.

5
4
3
1
2
6

Map of the Palace of Comares

Drawing by Ana Campos

1. ***Court of the Myrtles***
2. ***South portico***
3. ***North portico***
4. ***Room of the Ship***
5. ***Chamber of Ambassadors***
6. ***Royal Baths****

*The ROYAL BATHS, which are approached in our journey as an independent chapter after the palaces, actually belong to the Palace of Comares.

We have chosen to discuss them in a separate chapter, since, as a result of the Christian reforms and various restorations, this space suffered changes to its original configuration and access points.

Today, although they are generally closed to the public, they have their own external access point to the Palace of Comares.

Court of the Myrtles
Patio de los Arrayanes

As in all Muslim houses, but on a larger scale here (it is 37 meters long and 24 meters wide), the court is the core of daily life and the nucleus around which all of the palace's other rooms are arranged. The rectangular space is traversed by an enormous pool. It has been assigned many names over the course of its history; the most popular one comes from the masses of myrtles on either side. On its two shorter sides, there are two porticoed galleries that grant access to the most important rooms: the Room of the Ship and the Throne Room at the north, and, on the opposite side, the Pabellón Sur (South Pavilion). The two longer sides are lined with doors that open onto independent rooms on two floors; today, the precise function of these rooms is unknown, although the most probable conjecture is that they were used as dwellings.

The porticos are rendered ethereal by their light architecture: seven carved decorative arches set among *sebka*[1] panels rest along fine columns. Supported by these columns, in turn, are the pillars that support the linteled structures.

Behind the north portico rises the mass of the Tower of Comares; in the south, the gallery of upper floor arches. It is easy to imagine how, behind the windows'

NOTES

[1] *Sebka*: A decorative motif of Muslim origin that involves superimposed rows of interwoven rhombi, their edges curved or foliated, forming a kind of network or tapestry.

Court of the Myrtles, south portico.

Reflection of the Tower of Comares in the Court's pool

latticework, discrete glances would have observed the bustling life around the courtyard.

Here, the water becomes a mirror in which everything takes on a double dimension. Water! Source of life and symbol of the Muslim paradise, flowing gently toward the pool from the little fountains beneath the porticos' arcade. Still water, reflecting the sky and the architecture like a mirror: it is as if the columns of the porticoed galleries rise out of the water itself. In this tranquil, luminous place, the simplicity of the shapes, the water, and the vegetation are united.

Room of the Ship Sala de la Barca

The Room of the Ship is accessed through a pointed arch with plant motifs in its spandrels[2]. The jambs[3] of this entrance arch contain two richly engraved niches with tiles in the interior. Vessels filled with water or per-

fume were placed here as symbols of hospitality. This room is the antechamber to the Throne Room, also known as the Chamber of Ambassadors. Its name comes from the Arabic word *baraka,* meaning "blessing," which is repeatedly inscribed across the walls of this room. A skirting board made

[2] *Spandrels*: Each of the spaces left by a circle on being inscribed inside a square; the space between the arch and the lintel. They have a triangular shape and one of their sides is curved.

[3] *Jambs*: Each of the two vertical parts, on the sides of doors or windows, that supports the lintel or arch that closes them.

Room of the Ship

Chamber of Ambassadors

from different kinds of tiles covers the entire space. At the ends, behind the side arches, are two bedrooms. The current roof is a reproduction that closely resembles the original, which was completely burned in a fire in 1890.

Chamber of Ambassadors

Salón de Embajadores

This is the largest room in the entire palace. Built in the shape of a perfect cube, it is located inside the great Tower of Comares. Three of its four walls are lined with nine small bedrooms, arranged in threes, with windows open to the outside. These windows were originally covered with colored

Detail of one of the nine open bedrooms along the Chamber walls

Chamber of Ambassadors

panes. The wooden latticework that currently covers them is a recent substitute that helps us recreate the magical chiaroscuro atmosphere that would have enveloped the whole hall at the time.

The room reveals the magnificence and divine source of the sultan's power. Profusely decorated, it was initially polychrome from floor to ceiling. The ornamentation resembles large stucco tapestries hanging from the walls, and there are various models: shells, flowers, stars… Another of the walls' constant elements is the script on the plasterwork. Here, there are two kinds: kufic[4] and cursive[5].

Detail of the plasterwork covering the Chamber walls

[4] *Kufic*: A type of Arabic calligraphy, considered the very oldest in this language. It is characterized by its straight, angular appearance. It comes from the city of Kufa in Iraq and was the first to appear in architectural decoration. It was a cultured, more solemn script; for the most part, only scholars and imams knew how to read it.

In the Alhambra, we can find an example of this script above the ceramic skirting board in the Chamber of the Ambassadors.

[5] *Cursive*: An Arabic calligraphy that emerged after the Kufic variety, as the use of script became increasingly widespread. It is circular and flexible in nature, the letters bound together. It was originally used in official and administrative writings, but it gradually spread and was used in architectural ornamentation, coming to be the form of script that the majority of people knew (the majority of the people who could read and write, that is, as most of the overall population could not). Most of the inscriptions found in the Alhambra are of this variety.

Ceiling of the Chamber of Ambassadors

The four edges of the roof converging in this central dome symbolize the four rivers of Paradise.

There are seven crowns of stars moving concentrically toward the central dome. They represent each of the seven heavens through which the soul must ascend before reaching Paradise.

Drawing by Ana Campos, based on another by Leopoldo Torres Balbás [Archive of the Alhambra]

The lower part of the walls is decorated with tiles. The tiles in this room are very well conserved.

Both in the ceramic tiling and the plaster panels, figures are repeated through a set of geometric transformations, and, as in a kaleidoscope, the space expands toward the infinite and the mind goes with it....Geometric and plant shapes are alternated with inscribed bands that stretch around the hall, praising Yusuf I (its builder) and God, since "only to Him do power, glory, and eternity belong." The motto "Only Allaha is victorious" appears repeatedly on the walls of the room.

The current floor is not the original one. The original, which had to be redone after significant damage, was made of white and blue glazed ceramic. Only a small remnant of this kind of mosaic remains in the center of the hall.

The room is canopiedby a majestic wooden dome, a masterwork of Muslim carpentry, made of thousands of colored pieces that symbolize the cosmos and the idea of Islamic Paradise. There are seven crowns of concentric stars, representing each of the seven heavens the soul must pass through before reaching the central dome, the last level: Islamic Paradise. The four edges of the roof converging in this central dome symbolize the four trees or the four rivers of this Paradise that, as in the Old Testament, is an Eden or a garden.

Although the stucco of the walls and the dome have lost their polychromy and the light no longer seeps through the vivid panes of stained glass, we can still imagine the subtle, intimate atmosphere of this hall when, in the half-light, the sultan would receive his visitors from his seat on the royal throne.

Let's accept the help provided by the testimony of German traveler Jerónimo Münzer when, two years after the Christian conquest, he found these palaces within a fortress:

> *I do not believe that anything similar may be found in Europe, as it is all so magnificent, so exquisitely created, that not even he who gazes upon it may be certain that he is not in Paradise.*
>
> [JERÓNIMO MÜNZER, 1494-1495]

Decoration and Ornamentation (I):

Techniques, Resources and Decorative Elements of Islamic Architecture

Set of muqarnas and stuccos at the Lindaraja balcony

Just like the outer aspect of Islamic buildings is usually simple and even modest, with barely any motifs and decorative elements, the inside is usually richly decorated, sometimes from the floor to the ceiling, without leaving a single space empty. This contrast between the outside and inside is very evident in the architecture of northern Africa and Spain.

The reason is none other that the philosophy of life of the Muslim people, who lived most of their lives indoors, inside their homes and palaces. Moreover, some of the spaces inside Alhambra type palaces, the decoration is even richer than that of other Muslim monuments, with their walls covered and decorated from the floor to the ceiling, leaving no space empty. An example of this is the Ambassador hall or the Throne inside the tower of Comares. Is it possible that when the Nasrids from Granada were building the Alhambra, they already sensed that the Arabo-Andalusian civilization was at the end of its existence? Isn't the Alhambra the Muslim's "swan-song" at al-Ándalus, who suffocated by the growing pressure of Christian Kingdoms, decided to leave their living will at Granada? This said, lets now focus on the techniques, resources and decorative elements of Islamic architecture, highlighting that the variety and number of decorative elements used in Islamic-Spanish architecture has been lower *than that of other places, which may be a result of the political and geographical isolation of the Peninsula with respect to the rest of the Islamic world.* However, even though there is less variety of techniques and resources, the degree of virtuosity and perfection in their construction is exceptional. Let's take for instance the most important ones present in the walls and ceilings of the rooms of the Alhambra.

Stucco

Stucco is the most widely used decorative element in the Islamic world because it is cost effective, it can be easily moulded or carved and because it can be adapted to all architectural supports: Walls, pillars, vaults, etc. Stucco allowed craftsmen to cover surfaces that have been poorly and roughly finished, granting it a rich and perfect appearance as well as touch of architectural virtuosity. The basic material used to make the stucco is plaster mixed with other materials such as marble or alabaster dust, which provide it with consistency and solidity. The first step was to prepare a mass comprised of water and these materials. When said mass was mixed and with the right consistency, it was applied to the wall or surface to be covered, leaving it ready for sculpting or moulding decorative motifs. Once the surface plastered with stucco had the right consistency, it was sculpted. It could be accomplished directly, although normally a drawing was made first (for example using coal dust) on the surface to be sculpted.

A template was used with the decorative motif, which was superimposed on the wall or surface to be decorated. The last step was for the craftsman to patiently carve the drawn areas using a small chisel.

This technique was completely ac-

View of the stucco walls of the Ambassadors Hall

complished manually; it was a slow and arduous task. For this reason in Persia and Iraq and later in Spain, the "moulding" technique was used, which was quick, accurate and required less work. The difference resided in that the still soft plaster mixture was applied into wooden moulds containing the drawings and once dry, it was removed from the mould. The last process in both cases was the finish, which provided greater consistency, brightness and quality to the surface, giving it a coat of lime or other substance, depending on the final look you wished to achieve and the normal uses of each geographical area. Also in many cases, the finished surface was painted in different colours, which made the background and the drawings stand out even more. "The Alhambra is like a carved plaster palace, where stucco is not only used to cover the wall, but even to replace it. A clear example of this is the Courtyard of Lions, where the more than one hundred and thirty columns surrounding it are not used to support the loads transmitted by the arches, but to hold the fine carved stucco networks that run from one to another" [Dominique CLÉVENOT and Gérard DEGEORGE. *Islam Ornamentation*, p. 88].

Muqarnas

Muqarnas are prisms or polyhedrons that are normally made of wood or stucco, with their lower part cut into a concave shape. The remarkable peculiarity of the geometric compositions made with muqarnas is that they can be used to cover any type of surface and inverted space, which allows them to be used to decorate ceilings, shelves, arches, pendentives, etc.; however, its most surprising application is the decoration of ceilings such as those of the Two Sisters and Abencerrages halls, which are true marvels of this decorative specialty. Although these shapes are also applied to wood, they are normally made of stucco (plaster) as in the case of the Alhambra. Wooden moulds were used to make these. Craftsmen began working from the bottom up, applying the moulds that were filled with plaster. Once dry, the plaster was removed from the mould and was then carved and polished for its final finish. There are seven basic prismatic shapes susceptible of being grouped in many combinations that are very lively and complicated.

These muqarna ceilings are a mathematical prodigy since by using a combination of geometric figures we are able to completely fill a space without leaving any area empty. The vaults of these ceilings are usually shaped into an octagonal star. For example at the Alhambra we can find different uses of the muqarnas in the pendentives or tubes that sometimes support the wooden ceilings, like at the Room

Example of the different shapes and lights created by the combinations of muqarnas

of the Ship; or in the arches of some rooms like the Hall of the Kings or at the entrance to the Room of the Ship.

Wood

Another technique in which Muslims were experts was carpentry applied to architecture. Roof wings, lattices, doors and windows, etc. However, it is in ceilings where the use of wood as a decorative element is noteworthy and surprising. Cedar wood was typically used because it is highly ductile and resistant since it is not affected by the terrible woodworm. These works could basically be created in two ways: By either carving and sculpting the wood with geometric drawings or bows; using marquetry or inlaying techniques consisting of creating the drawings on the wood by stuffing smaller pieces of other woods such as ebony, lemon, sycamore, tinted woods, other materials such as shells, bones, ivory, mother of pearl, silver or other precious metals.

The final effect is a set of surprising shapes, colours and textures.

Inside the Alhambra we can see many examples of this; some of them are reproductions of the original ceilings that existed in the past.

The most important example is probably seen in the Hall of Ambassadors.

Ceramics

When talking about ceramics applied to decorating buildings, we are referring to tile or tiling, which are similar concepts although each of them has a different etymology: "azulejo" (tile) comes from the Arabic word "az-zulayan", which means glassy brick; "alicatado" (tiling) comes from the word

View of the wooden ceiling of the hallway communicating the Mexuar with the Comares Palace

"al-qata'a", which means "a piece of or cut tile". Alicatar (tiling) would be to cover a surface using pieces of cut tiles. Ceramic pieces used for decorating buildings first appeared between the XI and XII centuries, bringing about a revolution, although at first, few colours were available, mostly comprised of different tones of blue. Progressively, tile pieces became increasingly popular and the variety of colours used also increased, especially in countries of Northern Africa and Spain where this type of decorative technique became an authentic specialty, with geometrically perfect and surprising finishes. Tile usually covers the bottom part of walls, in combination with stucco, which decorates the upper part.

This decorative technique requires a long process that runs from the manufacturing of the pieces until the pieces are installed on the wall: The manufacturing process begins by making the paste, which was created by mixing clay with water, using rollers until a humid and plastic mixture was obtained.

Another step is the shaping of the standard parts required for making a specific motif. This shaping may be accomplished when the part is still soft, prior to it being baked, by applying the mass to moulds that give it shape, or by cutting the part when it is dry and cooked. The parts are dried and cooked in an oven or "mufla". Once cooked and prior to applying the varnish, the part is called "bizcocho".

Finally the part is varnished and coloured. The colours are achieved using oxides from different metals: Blue (cobalt), sapphire (copper dioxide), green (copper or chrome oxide), etc; each colour, depending on its brightness or finish required a specific baking, which requires the parts be placed back into the oven. Another interesting aspect is the symbols, which for Muslims are comprised of specific colours: Green is the colour of the prophet; curiously, all Muslim countries have this colour on their flag, especially the flag of Saudi Arabia, the cradle of Muhammad and Islam, which is completely green; yellow is the colour of the sun; blue is the colour of the sky, Paradise; red is the colour of blood, war or erotic ardour.

Regarding the placement and arrangement of the pieces, they were placed directly on the wall. Once the parts were silhouetted, either by cutting or applying moulds, they were filed down to fit perfectly in the motif they would then become part of.

When the pieces were cut using a ruler and chisel or using an "azulea", many would break, which made them very expensive. This is why it became standard to use steel moulds to shape the pieces when they were still soft. The small tiles are assembled one to another, upside down and on the floor or on a flat surface. When all the pieces are fitted, they are covered using mortar. When the mortar dries, the tiles form a single and flat block that is applied to the wall. The difficulty of some of the drawings and the small size of the pieces required great skill by part of the craftsman that was assembling it. When the surface to be covered is not flat but curved, the difficulty is even greater. In this case the tiles are assembled, not on the floor or a flat surface, but on concave surfaces with the shape of the wall or arch to be covered, and once the mortar joining them is dry, it is hoisted and attached. The difficulty also varies as a function of the drawing, the size and types of pieces that comprise it, as well as the manner in which these pieces are arranged.

In this regard, we could say that the Alhambra has two types of tiled baseboards: Ones, which drawing is comprised of two, three or four different medium or large sized pieces, prefabricated and previously moulded and installed next to each other forming a composition where you can easily differentiate each one of the geometric pieces that comprise the assembly (squares, triangles, stars, etc.), like for example the baseboards of the Court of the Myrtles [*Composition 1*]. The others, undoubtedly much harder to make, are those where the motif is formed by a large number of different pieces,

Composition 1

Composition 2

which are smaller and cross each other forming nets and an interconnection of geometric drawings, where it is more difficult to differentiate each one of the pieces that comprise the assembly, like for example those on the walls of the Hall of Ambassadors or the Hall of the Mexuar [*Composition 2*].

The Palace of the Lions

This palace was built by Muhammad V, a sultan who lost the throne for three years, although he would later recover it. It is the Alhambra's most universally recognized space.

The Palace of the Lions was built by Muhammad V (1354-1359 and 1362-1391), a sultan who lost the throne for three years and then recovered it. His long and fruitful reign — the product of an extended period of open peace, thanks to relationships marked by alliances and friendship with Pedro I de Castilla[1] (Peter I of Castile) — is linked to the Nasrid king-

NOTES

[1] *Aliance with Peter I*: Muhammad V, who had acceded to the throne at a very young age, was dethroned by his half-brother Ismail II — who, in turn, was murdered by Muhammad VI, the true instigator of the revolt that had caused him to lose the throne. In 1361, Muhammad V, supported by former members of his court in Granada, returned to the peninsula with the goal of regaining power. He estab-

Court of the Lions

lished a solid pact of alliance and vassalage with Peter I of Castile; together, they defeated Mohammad VI, thus recovering the Granadan throne. Like his friend and ally Muhammad V, Peter I of Castile had serious territorial disputes with Christian nobles and kings from other kingdoms on the Peninsula. Without a doubt, this was yet another reason to favor a policy of alliances and understanding with the Granandan king.

dom of Granada's era of greatest splendor. As in all large houses and palaces, the central space is occupied by a courtyard around which all the other rooms are arranged. The difference from other courts, however, is that this one has a fountain instead of a pool in the middle; the porticoed gallery that rings its entire perimeter is also different. It is consid-

Gallery of the Court of the Lions

ered to be the most private, intimate space of all. Along its longer sides are two independent dwellings, one in front of the other; along the shorter sides, two more open rooms that would have been used for different purposes depending on the necessities and events occurring at the time. Current access and internal movement among the different palaces constituting the sultan's house was a Christian development. As a result, this palace's entrance wasn't originally via the Court of the Myrtles, but rather the now nonexistent Lower Royal Street towards the southwestern area of the palace, very close to the Hall of the Muqarnas.

Corner of the Hall of the Kings

Map of the Palace of the Lions

Drawing by Ana Campos

1. ***Court of the Lions***
2. ***Hall of the Muqarnas***
3. ***Hall of the Abencerrages***
4. ***Hall of the Kings***
   4a. Side bedrooms with painted vaults
5. ***Hall of Two Sisters***
6. ***Hall of the Aljimeces***
7. ***Lindaraja Viewpoint***

7
6
5
1
4a
4
4a
4a
3

Court of the Lions Patio de los Leones

This is the most universally recognized space in the entire Alhambra, the most frequently sketched and photographed by travelers and visitors from all eras. In the middle of the court is a fountain with the twelve lions that lend the court, as well as the palace itself, its name. Much has been written about its symbology. Perhaps the most widespread interpretation is that it symbolizes "the bronze sea of Solomon's temple,"[2] represented by a large cup held up by twelve oxen (the number of the tribes of Israel), which, as described in the *Book of Kings*, resembled this fountain. In this case, lions, which represent

[2] King Solomon is an important figure in the three monotheistic religions: Islam, Judaism, and Christianity. The Muslims called Jews and Christians *Ahl al-kitab,* which means "people of the book" (the Bible, the Old Testament), of which even they incorporated some traditions and revelations prior to Muhammad. The three religions are related to Abraham. For them, King Solomon was a wise king and one of their prophets.

Detail of the Fountain of the Lions

Court of the Lions from the Hall of the Muqarnas

royal power, are the animals bearing the basin. Others believe that they represent the twelve months or the year or the twelve signs of the zodiac... Since they involve a number easily linked to different esoteric symbologies, interpretations are generally varied and open-ended.

Many theories have also existed about the historical era to which these lions belong; many believe the lions actually predate the basin they hold up. The basin itself dates, without a doubt, from the time of the court's construction: the fourteenth century. The theory that the lions are much older — from the tenth or eleventh century — is a very recent one.

Studies derived from the most recent restoration, carried out not long ago, are inclined to determine that they possibly date from the fourteenth century as well, and that they were commissioned along with the basin of the fountain. Its entire upper rim is engraved with a poem, written by the poet and statesman Ibn Zamrak. This poem extols Muhammad V and describes the lions' attitude and the beauty of the fountain and the water that spills from it.

As of the sixteenth century, the Christians changed the fountain's original configuration through successive interventions over time. They added a

The Court of the Lions, *1834. Etching according to David Roberts.*

second, smaller basin above the current one, as well as a large water jet, as can be seen in the oldest etchings and photographs of the court. In 1966, the fountain was restored to its original appearance.

Eastern gallery of the Court of the Lions

The entire court is a garden, an allegory of paradise, an oasis in which the 124 marble columns that border it — connected by arches and fine engraved stucco panels at their upper sections — may have symbolized a forest of palm trees. Some, on observing the porticoed gallery of aligned columns that surrounds the court, have also seen a Christian influence that evokes monastic cloisters. This idea is supported by Muhammad V's friendship and alliance with the Christian king Peter I, who in his own palace within the Alcázar of Seville, had previously constructed a court with many similarities to this one.

A channel of water emerges from each of the four lateral alcoves on the sides, flowing into the central fountain. These channels represent the four rivers of the Muslim Paradise, which divide the world — as the channels divide the court — into four parts. If we examine the old etchings and photographs, the surface[3] of the court has gradually changed over time. However, the latest intervention conducted by the Council of the Alhambra has returned this space to its original appearance, which, it is believed, was covered in marble stone.

[3] The court's paving has changed over time, from the Christian conquest through the present day. To increase its image as a "garden," one of the interventions undertaken by the monument's conservators planted flowers all over the central part, believing that this had been its original appearance. However, the latest research tends to conclude that the entire surface would have been made of marble.

General view of the Court of the Lions

Hall of the Muqarnas
Sala de los Mocárabes

The palace's old entrance from the outside was once located here, which is why, it is thought, this space had a clear purpose as a vestibule or entrance hall. Since it was not configured as a dwelling, it must have had a more versatile function — which also would have been the case for the hall in front of this one, on the other side of the court. Its name comes from the muqarnas work on the vaulted ceiling that covered the entire room and which was seriously damaged after a nearby powder keg explosion in 1590; it then had to be demolished.

During this phase, the hall was divided by a grille that differentiated the spaces between right and left. The plaster vault that occupies part of the roof corresponds to one of these parts. It was created on the occasion of Felipe V's (Phillip V) visit to the Alhambra with his wife, Isabel de Parma, in the early eighteenth century. The three large muqarna arches that open onto the court are the most important and best-preserved decorative element in the whole hall.

Hall of the Abencerrages
Sala de los Abencerrajes

This space, on the south side of the court, was designed to be a private dwelling. It had a wooden door that gave it a certain independence from the court. At the entrance to the hall, there is a small transversal passage with a door on each side. The right-hand door leads to the upper floor; the latrine[4] is behind the left-hand door. The source of the

[4] *Latrine*: Muslim houses began to be outfitted with latrines much earlier than in the West. The latrine was one of the few spaces within the house that had a single, differentiated purpose, since the rooms in Muslim houses fulfilled various purposes throughout the day. People sought to isolate them as much as possible from the rest of the house, using walls or wall-bends, and they tended to be located as close as possible to the street or courtyard. The latrine was ventilated; it was also typically equipped with a small basin or sink. It generally had a rectangular surface, elevated over the surface of the floor, with a long, narrow groove in the middle.

Hall of the Muqarnas

Hall of the Abencerrages

hall's name is that here, as the legend goes, members of the powerful lineage of Abencerrages were beheaded. The space is laid out across a central hall and two small lateral chambers, designed for resting. A small fountain occupies the center of the hall, reflecting the roof's beautiful muqarna dome. In the shape of an eight-pointed star, it represents the canopy of heaven, a new

Ceiling of the Hall of the Abencerrages

allegory of Paradise. It is unarguably one of the Alhambra's most important decorative elements. The light trickles in through the upper latticework and softly illuminates the entire space. The tiles of the skirting board on the lower section aren't originals; they come from Seville's tile factory and were put in place during the sixteenth century.

Hall of the Kings

Sala de los Reyes

This hall is located on the east side of the court. It is a long space, measuring over 30 meters. Given its large scale, it is believed that the room was probably reserved for parties and receptions or as a meeting space. The Catholic Monarchs used it as a chapel. The rectangular space that constitutes the hall is divided into three large square bedrooms and two smaller ones — one on each side — at the ends. The three large central rooms are separated by sections of double muqarna arches and are canopied by lanterns and independent coverings. Each one has a muqarna dome. All of the walls are decorated with tile squares and the characteristic plasterwork that lines most of this palace's rooms.

Around the entire hall, along the opposite side of the patio, are five bedrooms. The three central ones contain highly unique paintings on their vaults, made on the leather that covers the wooden vaults. They have been heavily studied, and it is believed that they were produced by Christian artists. These paintings are yet another example of the special Christian-Muslim fusion taking place during this era, when the cross-border influence and cultural "contagion" among the kingdoms' inhabitants was the order of the day.

Of the paintings on these three vaults, the ones on the central vault portray ten noble or illustrious

Hall of the Kings

Detail of the skirting board in the Hall of the Kings

Paintings on leather in the Hall of the Kings

Muslims conversing. For a time it was thought — erroneously, it would seem — that they were sultans from the Nasrid dynasty, and the name of the hall comes from this belief. The paintings on the other two vaults depict chivalresque scenes combining Muslim and Christian figures.

Hall of Two Sisters
Sala de Dos Hermanas

Like the Hall of Abencerrages, this hall was also a residence; it is the primary and most important space in the whole palace. It was closed off by

a large wooden door that can now be viewed at the Museum of the Alhambra. Like the other dwelling, it is preceded by a small transversal passage with doors on both sides. Like the other one, too, one door leads to the latrine and the other to the stairs reaching the upper floor bedrooms. It owes its name to the two large marble slabs that pave the floor of the main hall. The space is laid out around a small circular fountain; a small water channel runs out of it and flows into the court fountain. It also has two side bedrooms with open windows, where the beds would have been. The left-hand bedroom has a door connected to the chambers commissioned by Charles V. Originally, this dwelling had its own garden, open to the northern rampart and offering beautiful views. Various modifications were made to this garden after Charles V's visit.

Its rich decoration makes this one of the most important spaces in the entire monument. Both for the stucco panels that completely cover its walls and for the tile skirting board below, it is among the most

Hall of the Two Sisters

Ceiling of the Hall of the Two Sisters

beautiful and best preserved of any we will find here. Above the skirting board, a poem by Ibn Zamrak runs around the entire room. This poem addresses Muhammad's greatness and describes the beauty of this work: "Such pleasure for the eyes! In this place the soul shall find a stunning dream." The most striking decorative element is, once again, the fabulous domed ceiling in the honeycombed muqarna style.

Next is the Sala de los Aljimeces (Hall of the Aljimeces), a small, long room, canopied by a muqarnavault, which serves as the transition to the Lindaraja Viewpoint.

What delicious perspectives are contained in my enclosure!
How many objects that, just by beholding them,
are enough to satisfy the demands
of a superior glory!

Look at this dome; its elegant proportions
darken and diminish all other domes.

The constellations reach their hands
towards it in a gesture of greeting; the full moon
itself abandons its course to speak with it.

[IBN ZAMRAK. Excerpt from some of the verses written along the walls of the hall.]

Detail of the plasterwork in the Hall of the Two Sisters

Detail of one of the skirting boards in the Hall of the Two Sisters

Lindaraja Viewpoint
Mirador de Lindaraja

This is a small quarter separated from the Hall of Two Sisters by the Hall of the Aljimeces, which, judging by its name (it comes from the Arabic words *al-Ayn Dar Aisa,* or "the eyes of Aisa's house"), must have been designated for the sultan's favorite woman. The view from this lookout was certainly different in Nasrid times. It opens onto the garden (which no longer exists), the Darro valley, and the Albaicín.

On the lower part, the tile skirting board displays small mosaics forming geometric stars. As is true of the Hall of Two Sisters, it is one of the richest and most carefully conserved spaces in the Alhambra. It is an example, as is the entire Palace of the Lions, of a period of peace and wealth experienced by the Kingdom of Granada. The skirting board that covers the jambs of the entry arch merits explicit mention because of the epigraphic inscriptions

Lindaraja Viewpoint from the Hall of the Two Sisters

on the ceramic of its upper part — highly uncommon in the Alhambra. The windows are low, as required by the Muslim custom of sitting on the floor on cushions or ottomans. The ceiling is formed by a wooden vault with colored glass embedded into it, recently restored; this is the only feature of its kind that has been conserved.

Decoration and Ornamentation (II):

Most Frequent Decorative Themes and Motifs

If there is any one item that characterizes the decoration of Islamic building, it is the existence of a series of common and almost constant decorative themes or motifs that are uniformly repeated regardless of the decorative technique or material that is used. These great decorative motifs are three: Epigraphic, vegetal and geometric.

Epigraphic motifs

Although in other cultures epigraphic motifs did not become decorative art, with the exception of Christian manuscripts and a few other isolated examples, in Islamic civilization, the use of writing as a decorative motif was able to establish a sublime base. The writing on Islamic buildings does not only serve a decorative purpose but also an iconographic one, comparable to and substitutive of the function of images in the Christian world. Its purpose is to conserve and manifest God's word. It is normally used to structure surfaces, for example using a strip to separate the union of the wall's tiled baseboard from the top portion of the wall, which is covered in stucco; or to frame a window, the curve of an arch or a portico. Two types of writings can be found:

- *Kufic*: It is characterized by having a straight and angular form; it originates from the word Kufa, in Iraq and it is the first one to appear in architectural decoration. It is an educated writing, which could only be read by scholars and Imams (priests). At the Alhambra it is found over the tile of the Ambassador Hall.
- *Cursive*: That shown on this page. It appears on the architectural ornamentation after the XII Century. It is a type of writing that has a linked nature and an almost circular and flexible shape, which at first was only used for official and administrative writings; however its use becomes generalized, becoming the standard used in architectural ornamentation since it is known by most people (most of the people who knew how to read since a large part of the population was illiterate).

Almost all the inscriptions of the Alhambra are of this type. By its content, most of the writings that adorn the walls of buildings are passages from the Koran. The entire Alhambra is full of religious writings such as the *leit motiv* "ONLY ALLAH IS VICTORIOUS", which is repeated to infinity. Writings

of an informative or historic nature are also present, which provide information about the meaning of the building, the date it was built or the persons who built it. Also very frequent at the Alhambra, although extremely rare in Islam prior to the XIV century are poems. These poems are songs praising the palace itself, the sultans or make symbolic allegories.

The two most illustrious poets of the Nasri monument are Ibn Zamrak, the most important, and Ibn Yayyab.

Vegetal motifs

Although vegetal decoration already existed in the pre-existing arts, in Islamic decorative arts it progressed from being used as a secondary motif to occupying a central place and playing a major role decorating large surfaces and even entire walls. This look towards everything represented by nature can be explained by their religious faith, through continuous references in the Koran regarding Paradise, which is defined as "The garden of Happiness". Vegetal decoration can be classified in two large groups. The first would be comprised of items that could be classified as having "the purist naturalism": Flowers, plants, trees, pines, shells, etc. The walls of the Alhambra are full of these types of motifs, like for example those on the mitral arches at the entrance to the Boat Hall, which has five trees etched at each side of the arch, each with their trunk, their different leaves and fruits, representing the gardens of Eden. Another item that appears frequently, and maybe the most important one, is the shell, which symbolize water, the blessing and work of Allah. These shells can be found everywhere. However, the most important symbols are found at oratories such as those of the Mexuar and el Partal, where whels always appear in threes, crowning the Mihrab. The other type of vegetal decoration, which could be classified as having an "abstract naturalism", is the arabesque, where the vegetal forms are distorted, becoming a repetitive and geometric motif. The arabesque is a "geometric" drawing, where the main item is a stem, which gradually expands into

Arabesque detail with intercalated pineapples and shells in the Court of the Lions and in the mihrab in the Oratory of the Partal

a continuous line, making unlimited turns throughout the entire surface of the drawing. This stem is divided into a series of secondary and thick stems, from which leaves, palmettes or clusters are born and used to fill the empty space. The symmetry and harmony with which the arabesque covers the spaces is based on the same mathematical principles that govern pure geometric decoration. At some places, this type of drawing achieves a type of abstraction where the main stem disappears, consisting of an overlapping of apparently vegetal leaves or motifs, which in a dynamic and rhythmic manner cover the entire space. The arabesque is one of the most frequent motifs in stuccos decorating the walls of the Alhambra.

Geometric motifs

Muslims inherited the use of geometric motifs applied to the decorating of buildings in classic architecture; however, they perfected these and gave them a degree of complexity and development that was previously unknown, turning them into the geometric decoration in a leading artistic mode. While geometric motifs appear in all the materials used in architectural ornamentation (stucco, wood, brick, etc.), it is in the covering of walls using ceramic pieces (tile or tile pieces) where they achieve a more important role.

Hidden in the decorative motifs that adorn the tile pieces at the Alhambra are geometric irregularities based on repetitive figures, colours that maintain a drawing pattern and geographic transformations such as symmetries, rotations or movements.

Decorative geometry helps to achieve very different perceptions. The repetition of motifs widens the space to infinity. The different ways to perceive the configurations of figures, depending on how we focus our eyesight, invite us to look at them again and again surprising us with new images seen in the same tile pieces.

The symmetry of the shapes can be perceived as being orderly and harmonious. Well articulated colour and the geometry stimulate the imagination and the enjoyment of the aesthetics. Underlying to these techniques there is always a solution to a classic problem in geometry: What geometric figures can cover a surface by placing them next to each other, without leaving any empty spaces and not overlapping them?

Let's analyze some of the most representative drawings of the Alhambra.

One of the most representative configurations known as "la pajarita" (baby bird), we find, among other places, in some of the baseboards of the Arrayanes Courtyard. The space is structured using identical equilateral triangles. The basis is always a triangle,

Figure 1

r a p h i c

Ceramic detail in the Hall of the Tower of the Ladies

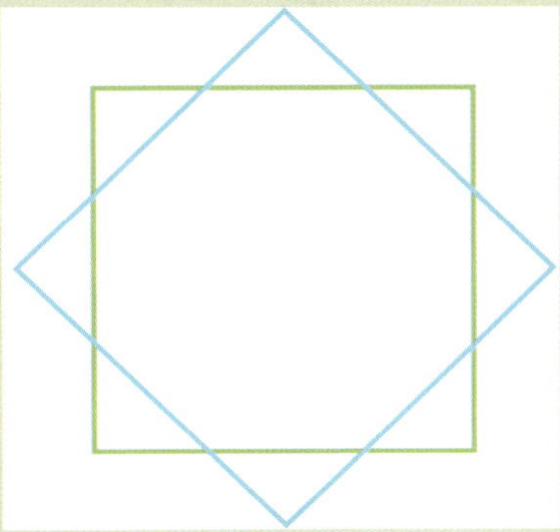

Figure 2a

Figure 2b

which is modified by intersecting it using three circular segments. These segments are positioned to maintain the original surface of the triangle. This is how the final form of this baby bird is obtained. A six point star and a hexagon placed in an alternating fashion in the centre complete the configuration. *Figure 1* is a graphic drawing of the final assembly.

Another shape that appears frequently is the star, which can be found in numerous combinations (stars with 8 points, 16 points or more), created by rotating squares. Let's take for example a star with 8 points, which is created by rotating a square with a 45° angle [*Figure 2a*]. The small squares that make up each large square are used as a guide for drawing the figures that comprise the star and the links of the drawing [*Figure 2b*]. The final composition, as shown in the photograph that accompanies the figures, may combine stars with different number of points, assembled to each other forming a network, where the link is the decorative motif that unifies and runs along the entire drawing. The final print forms a kind of non-ending labyrinth comprised of multiple coloured shapes, which viewed as a whole show a different perspective of the geometric landscape.

THE PALACES
The Christian Rooms

were designed as lodging for the Emperor Charles V and Empress Isabel in their future visits to Granada following their first stay in the city.

View of the Albaicín from the gallery of the Queen's Robing Room

When the Catholic Monarchs entered the Alhambra in 1492, they were stunned by the beauty of the Nasrid Palaces — to such an extreme that they established their residence here for their visits to Granada, henceforth dubbing these palaces "Casa Real de la Alhambra" (Royal House of the Alhambra). From the very beginning, they undertook projects to modify as they pleased and preserve what would be, from then on, properties of their crown.

When their grandson Charles V came to Granada in 1526 after his wedding, he stayed in the Alhambra and was equally struck by the place. Thus, in 1528, he commissioned somechambers here as lodging for the Emperor and his family during their trips to Granada.

These building works transformed what had previously been some gardens, open to the ramparts in an enclosed space, composed of two adjacent courts and their respective galleries. Also undertaken in this area, in the upper part of the ancient tower named for Abu Hayyay (Yusuf I), was the construction of yet another room dedicated to Empress Isabel.

Charles V had a much larger and more ambitious plan to execute in the Alhambra: the construction of a great Renaissance palace that would bear his name. However, even though the work to build this new palace would be expensive and certainly not brief, the new spaces would fulfill their purpose as soon as construction was finished.

Upper gallery of the Court of the Lindaraja

Map of the Christian Rooms

Drawing by Ana Campos

1. ***Emperor's Chambers:***
   1a. Emperor's Office
   1b. Washington Irving's rooms
   1c. Halls of Fruits
2. ***Court of the Grated Window***
3. ***Court of Lindaraja***
4. ***Queen's Robing Room***

4
1b
1b
1c
1c
3

Room in the Office of the Emperor.
This is the first of the six spaces that constitute the Christian Rooms.

Habitaciones del Emperador

As part of the building plan that followed Emperor Charles V's first visit to the Alhambra, six rooms were commissioned: rooms that, although austere, were more in accordance with the lifestyle and habitability of Western spaces. Curiously, once they were finished, these new spaces were never used either by the Emperor or by his wife.

They are accessed through a hallway that begins in one of the lateral rooms of the Hall of Two Sisters. The first is known as the room of the "Despacho del Emperador" (Emperor's Office); noteworthy elements are the large chimney and the paneled roof with the motto *Plus Ultra* and the imperial initials K and Y (Karolo and Ysabel). Next is a room that serves as a hall for the spaces. To the right, the four rooms that complete this body of chambers, envisioned as bedrooms for the Emperor and Empress. They are also known as "Washington Irving's rooms,"[1] with reference to the author of

NOTES

[1] Washington Irving was born in New York City in 1783. A diplomat, historian, and traveler, he reached Granada in the spring of 1829. He lived for some time in the Alhambra itself, which was inhabited at the time. Inspired by its walls, by his neighbors' voices, and by the Muslim chroniclers, he wrote his now-universal tales, halfway between history and legend. The success of this work drew travelers and artists from other countries to Granada, ready to discover the beauty and the magic of all the places Irving had described.

One of the spaces envisioned as a bedroom for the emperors

One of the two Halls of Fruits

Tales of the Alhambra, who lived in them in 1829. They look out onto the north of the Court of Lindaraja, the upper part. The first two rooms are larger than the second two, which are known as "Salas de Frutas" (Halls of Fruits) because of the drawings on their roofs. These drawings are the work of Julio Aquiles and Alejandro Mayner.

Courts of the Grated Window and of Lindaraja

Patios de la Reja y de Lindaraja

Court of the Grated Window, also known as the Court of the Cypresses.

These two beautiful courts, one right beside the other, emerged from the modifications undertaken in this part of the Alhambra in order to build Charles V's chambers.

The first court, the Court of the Grated Window, is accessed through an air corridor built in the Christian era that showcases a beautiful panorama — spanning the Albaicín, the Sacromonte, and the Darro valley. It is a quiet, elegant Italian-style court with a small fountain in the middle. Its name comes from the wrought iron grille, serving as a balcony, that runs along the upper part of the southern wall. It is also known as the Patio de los Cipreses (Court of the Cypresses) due to the four hundred-year-old trees of this species that adorn it.

The second court is located just below the Lindaraja Viewpoint, which lends it its name. The porticoed galleries of its lower section were built with columns brought from other places in the Alhambra. Charles V's rooms are located in the upper section. A small fountain of Christian design sits in the center. The white marble basin of the upper part is of Nasrid origin and was replaced by a replica in 1995 so that it could be restored.

Court of Lindaraja

Small gallery that surrounds the Robing Room

Queen's Robing Room

Peinador de la Reina

The Queen's Robing Room from its entrance gallery

This quiet space is the result of the alterations carried out on the upper part of the old Abu Hayyay (Yusuf I) Tower in 1537, as part of the interventions scheduled after Charles V's first visit to the Alhambra. The objective of these works was to fit out the space for the Empress Isabel's enjoyment — who, it seems, never ultimately inhabited them. Years later, Isabel de Parma, Phillip V's wife, did stay in this room. Irving dedicated one of his stories — "Legend of the Rose of the Alhambra,"[2] among the loveliest — to that visit, King Phillip, and his wife.

[2] *Legend of the Rose of the Alhambra*:

In this story, a beautiful but lowly young orphan girl, who lived with her aunt in one of the Alhambra's towers, falls desperately in love with a page in the service of Queen Isabel de Parma, whom she met when the Monarchs stayed in the Alhambra during their visit to Granada. At the end of the story, the beautiful young woman — brought to the court by Queen Isabel herself — uses her singing and the magical notes of a lute to cure King Phillip, sick with melancholy and sorrow. Thanks to this recovery and the Queen's favors, she ends up marrying the very same kind and handsome young man with whom she had fallen in love, years before, in the Alhambra.

Ceiling of the Robing Room

The upper part of this tower, altered by the Christians, has a hall or antechamber that grants access to a small room, the dressing room. The dressing room floor has been removed, returning this space to its original function as a lantern. Outside, surrounding the dressing room or lantern, is a beautiful gallery, also accessed through the first antechamber. The walls are decorated with frescoes by the Italian painters Julio Aquiles and Alejandro Mayner, which portray scenes of Charles V's expedition against Tunisia (in the antechamber) and mythological scenes, cherubs, floral figures, and small animals (in the dressing room).

Antechamber of the Robing Room

THE PALACES
Royal Baths

These baths belonged to the Palace of Comares and, after conquest, were conserved and equipped for use by the Catholic Monarchs — unlike the rest of the Alhambra's baths, which were destroyed.

PAGE

Elevation of the Baths, according to a drawing by Owen Jones, 1842-1845.

Built during the reign of Yusuf I (1333-1354), they are known as the "Baños del Palacio de Comares" (Baths of the Palace of Comares) because they belonged to that palace. They were originally accessed through one of the palace's chambers. For Muslims, the bath was a religious obligation, as the Koran requires bodily cleanliness to achieve spiritual cleanliness. The bath was also a place of social harmony. A medieval Muslim city is inconceivable without baths. There were many in the Alhambra: some public — like the one that was located beside the Mosque, which still exists and may be visited — and others private. All of the Alhambra's important palaces were equipped with their own baths[1].

Muslims organized their baths based on the structure of the Roman thermal baths, although with various small modifications. They are normally divided into four rooms, as is also true in Roman baths. The first, the *apoditerium*, is a dry room, designed for changing one's clothes or staying to rest after

IMMERSION ROOM OVEN

bathing. The other three, *frigidarium*, *tepidarium*, and *caldarium*, would be the wet rooms, or, precisely put, the baths — with water, high temperatures, and steam. The major difference is found in the *frigidarium*, or cold room: in the Alhambra, this would have been, more than a room, a kind of vestibule without a pool (which the Roman *frigidarium* did have). Instead, it would have been be a small basin for performing ablutions. The Christians made some changes later, adapting these spaces to their own intended purposes and opening up several doors. This would have been unthinkable in its initial state, as it would have weakened the original isolation of the Muslim bath — necessary in order to avoid the loss of hot air and to protect intimacy.

NOTES

[1] By assessing the archaeological remains that have been discovered over time, it is now known that there were baths in all of the Alhambra's important palaces; examples include the Alcazaba, the Generalife, the Palace of Yusuf III, and even the Palace of the Lions. Nearly all of the baths have vanished; after conquest, they were prohibited by Royal Decree, as the Christians considered them a symbol of Muslim religious practices.

These baths in the Palace of Comares have survived because, as they were part of their new Royal House, the Christian kings modified them for their own use. The public baths of the Mosque (Baths of the Polinario) have also been preserved because they were hidden inside a modern dwelling. Once the home was torn down, the baths were exposed almost in their entirety.

Rest Room

Rest Room
Apoditerium

Public baths did not include a rest room — or at least not with the significance and lavishness that characterizes them in these Royal Baths. Here, a visitor proceeded to undress when the bath began. Once it was over, he would return to rest. The room contained two beds or divans on both sides, which would have been covered at the time with cushions and tapestries.

Peculiarly, the spacehas two floors. According to tradition, in the upper gallery, groups of musicians or singers would recite poetry or play instruments. It is one of the most thoroughly restored rooms in the Alhambra, and although many of its original elements are maintained, it has perhaps been slightly distorted by the excess of color that was used to repaint its stucco walls.

Cold Room
Frigidarium

This is not an authentic *frigidarium*; rather, it serves as a kind of vestibule or transition/acclimation area before entering the hotter rooms. It does not have the cold-water pool that Roman thermal baths contained. Instead, there is a small basin that was used for partial ablutions.

Steam Room
Tepidarium

In medieval times, this room had to be kept closed so that steam wouldn't escape; for that reason, the door currently found in the wall wouldn't have existed. This is the central room, the longest space, and the most important bath of the set. Among its standout elements are the star-shaped chandeliers on its vaulted ceiling; they may have originally been canopied by colored glass. Water ran along channels on the floor and, as the marble was heated

Steam Room

by underground conduits, steam was abundantly produced in the air. On each side, separated from the central space by triple arcades, is a room in which the bathers would presumably sit or lie down to receive a massage.

Immersion Room

Caldarium

Adjoined to the wall of the oven, this room would reach the highest

temperatures. The hypocaust coursed beneath it, an underground channel through which hot air circulated as it flowed out of the oven and heated the floor of the entire *caldarium*. This is why the bathers used thick-soled footwear to protect their feet as they moved around, as the floor could reach high temperatures. There are two compartments in this room, each one containing a basin: one with hot water that was supplied by the heater and another with hot water. The right-hand basin was known as the "Baño de la Sultana" (Bath of the Sultana); the left-hand basin, larger, the "Baño del Sultán" (Bath of the Sultan). This one displays a niche with an inscription dedicated to Yusuf I.

Oven Rooms

The oven rooms were located on the other side of this space's southern wall — a much thinner partition so that the heat could be transmitted. These rooms were cut off from the rest of the baths: not only to prevent the steam from reaching the other bathing areas, but also so that the oven workers, woodcutters, and other people not working at the service of the palace couldn't enter this deeply intimate space. Additionally, the bustling tasks required to fuel the heater with wood would rupture the atmosphere of silence and tranquility that must be maintained in the bathing rooms. These rooms were accessed from outside the palace, through the now nonexistent "woodcutters' street."

Bath of the Sultan in the Immersion Room

The Partal and the Towers

This space was occupied by beautiful residencies where some of the Alhambra's most distinguished families made their home. Here, too, are the most beautiful towers that, with their incredible interior beauty, are like small palaces.

The Partal Gardens. In the background, the Tower of the Ladies.

NOTES

[1] *Palace of Yusuf III*: Built by Yusuf III. Although only archeological remnants are left to us today, it is known to have been one of the Alhambra's largest and most important palaces. In the Christian era, the Catholic Monarchs ceded it to the first governor of the Alhambra, Sir Íñigo de Mendoza: Count of Tendilla and Marquis of Mondéjar.

How could a building of such beauty and magnitude just disappear

In Nasrid times, this space was filled with noble residences and beautiful palaces inhabited by the Alhambra's most distinguished families. A large number of these edifices have disappeared; in the early twentieth century, the Partal Gardens were designed over their archaeological remains. The result is a delightful, peaceful backwater, a place of calm for every visitor. In the upper part are the remains of the Palace of Yusuf III[1], which, after the Christian conquest, was the residence of the fortress's governors.

Here, too, begins the route that will lead us toward the Generalife, where the Alhambra's most beautiful and legendary towers are located, oriented toward the Albaicín: authentic palace residences designed more for dwelling and enjoying the landscape than for defense.

— almost entirely? The explanation lies in the fact that, when the succession conflict arose between the Bourbons and the Austrians over the Spanish crown, the Count of Tendilla's descendants gave their support to the House of the Austrians. Consequently, when the Bourbons finally assumed the throne, they divested this noble Granandan family of governorship of the Alhambra, as well as their possession of this palace, as an act of reprisal. Before abandoning the palace, the furious Tendillas decided to destroy it so that no one else could live there.

The Tower of the Ladies and the Albaicín

THE PARTAL AND THE TOWERS

Drawing by Carlos Quintanilla

1. ***Tower of the Ladies***
2. ***Oratory***
3. ***Tower of the Pointed Battlements***
4. ***Tower of the Cadí***
5. ***Tower of the Captive***
6. ***Tower of the Infants***
7. ***Remnants of the Palace of Yusuf III***

4
5
6

Palace of the Partal or Tower of the Ladies

Palacio del Partal o Torre de las Damas

The Palace of the Partal (portico) lends its name to this entire space. It is the Alhambra's very oldest palace, dating from the time of Muhammad III (1302-1309). A tower with a five-arched porticoed gallery and a pool are the elements that help us identify what would have been a palace in its day. Since the sixteenth century, it has also been known as the Tower of the Ladies.

There are three clearly differentiated spaces: the PORTICOED GALLERY, where we should pay special attention to its wooden roof; the HALL, at the rear, with its exceptional tiled skirting boards along the lower part of the walls; and the UPPER OBSERVATION POINT with plasterwork that is especially valuable for its beauty and age. The lookout's ceiling, dome-shaped and made of engraved wood, is a copy. The original can be found in Berlin's Islamiches Museum. This space is generally closed to the public.

Some small Arab houses and a lovely oratory border the remains of this palace. Nearby is the Rauda, or the royal cemetery of the Nasrid dynasty.

Remnants of the Palace of the Partal. Since the sixteenth century, it has also been known as the Tower of the Ladies.

Oratory of the Partal

Detail of the portico in the Tower of the Ladies

Pool and Gardens of the Partal

Window of the
Tower of the Pointed Battlements

Tower of the Pointed Battlements

Torre de los Picos

Seen from the outside, this is the most peculiar of all the towers in the Alhambra because of the battlements (corbels), shaped like the points of its name, on the terrace. It was built at the end of the thirteenth century or the beginning of the fourteenth. It has three sections and, judging by the interior decoration of one of its floors, it may fit within the typology of tower-dwellings. The tower protected and was integrated into the Gate of the Arrabal, one of the two access routes into the precincts along the northern flank, a crossing and natural exit toward the Generalife.

The Christians expanded it after conquest, building an exterior bastion and some stables, keeping the tower and the gate as part of the interior; they used the gate of the bastion, called Puerta de Hierro (Iron Gate), as the outer gate.

Tower of the Pointed Battlements

*Bastions and stables.
Christian edifices,
outside the Tower.*

View from inside the Tower

Decorative motif on one of the windows

Lower floor

Remnants of paintings on the ceiling of the upper floor

Tower of the Captive

Torre de la Cautiva

This is like a small palace inside a tower. Its structure is quite similar to any other dwelling in the Alhambra, with an upper floor and a terrace. It was built in the thirteenth century, although its interior decoration and its configuration as a residence correspond to the time of Yusuf I (1333-1354), as can be deduced from inscriptions in the main room.

The Tower of the Captive from the Promenade of the Towers

Its current name comes from the fact that, as the legend goes, the Christian lady Isabel de Solís[2] lived here as a captive, who, over time, would convert to Islam and become the favorite of Abu l-Hasan Ali.

The most noteworthy element of its interior is the profuse stucco decoration of the walls and its tiled skirting boards — among the few that have ceramic inscriptions on its upper friezes.

[2] Isabel de Solís was a Christian maiden, daughter of the knight commander of Martos, Sir Sancho Jiménez de Solis. Particularly in the border areas between the Christian and Muslim kingdoms, ambushes and military actions were very common at the time — whether to conquer territories or simply to attack towns, plunder, and take captives so as to demand ransom from their families. This maiden was captured by Nasrid soldiers and brought to the Alhambra as a captive. She was so beautiful that the sultan Abu l-Hasan Ali fell in love with her. She converted to Islam with the name Zoraya (morning star) and they married. Their marriage incurred the jealousy of and political struggles with the sultan's first wife, previously his favorite: Aixa, mother of Boabdil. So great were the tensions and intrigues in the court as a result of this relationship with a former Christian that Abu l-Hasan Ali, who no longer had the people's support, ultimately abdicated in favor of his brother, al Zagal, who was much more popular than he.

When the Catholic Monarchs seized Granada, Zoraya was exiled with her husband and children. It would appear that she re-converted to Catholicism after Abu l-Hasan Ali's death.

Detail of the plasterwork inside the Tower

Inside the Tower of the Captive

Inscriptions on ceramic along the skirting boards of the walls

Inside the Tower of the Captive

Decorative motifs on one of the windows

Tower of the Infants

Torre de las Infantas

This is also a tower-palace, very similar in structure to the Tower of the Captive, with an upper floor and a terrace. It is one of the final works under-

taken in the Muslim Alhambra, from the time of Muhammad VII (1392-1408), corresponding to a now-decadent period in the Nasrid reign, as reflected in a much simpler style of decoration. The central space is occupied by a court with a small fountain; three adjacent rooms are distributed around it. The upper floor is barely decorated. It originally had a muqarna ceiling, but it was destroyed by an earthquake in the nineteenth century and replaced with the current wooden ceiling.

The origin of its contemporary name is that, according to the legend of "The Three Beautiful Princesses"[3] described by Washington Irving in his *Tales of the Alhambra,* three Arab princesses lived in this tower: Zaida, Zoraida, and Zorahaida.

[3] The legend of "The Three Beautiful Princesses":

According to this legend, there was a Moorish king in Granada, called "el Zurdo" (left-handed) by his subjects, who had three daughters. Astrologers informed the king that, once grown, his daughters would be so beautiful that it would be wise to keep them away from masculine eyes and instincts. Thus, he made the daughters live far from the court, in the Castillo (Castle) of Salobreña. When they had become women of marrying age, he brought them to the Alhambra, where they lived in near confinement in the Tower of the Infants. Although they were surrounded by luxuries, their only company was that of an old woman carer and they felt very unhappy. Fate determined, however, that one day they fell in love with three brave, handsome Christian knights, who were being held as prisoners by their father in hopes that their rich families would pay a ransom. The story ends with two of the princesses escaping to Christian lands with the noble knights.

Exterior of the Tower of the Infants among the Generalife gardens

Niche at the entrance of one of the Tower's bedrooms

General view of the Tower interior

Detail of the ceramic skirting boards

*Windows along the upper floor and ceiling of the Tower.
This wooden ceiling is a reconstruction;
the original one was made of muqarnas.*

View of the towers and the Albaicín

Charles V, the Great Western Emperor

Charles I of Spain and V of the Holy Roman Empire was born on the 24th of February, 1500 in Gante. By way of the arranged marriages policy, which in the day was planned by his grandparents for his children, he inherited a large number of kingdoms and territories, not only in Europe but also in America. His mother was Princess Joanna, daughter of the Catholic Kings, Isabella I of Castile and Fernando II of Aragon. His father was Archduke Philip, Son of Maximilian I of Habsburg, Emperor of the Holy Roman Empire and Mary of Burgundy.

But there was also another circumstance that came into play regarding this figure since sometimes due to premature deaths like that of his father, and other times for health reasons (his mother was incapacitated by his grandfather Ferdinand), he came to power and governed these territories at a very young age; in some cases when he was a teenager.

From his paternal grandmother Mary of Burgundy he inherited the Netherlands. From his paternal grandfather Maximilian of Habsburg, he inherited the German Empire and its territories. From his maternal grandfather Ferdinand of Aragon, the Kingdom of Aragon and the Italian conquests of Sardinia, Naples and Sicily. From his maternal grandmother Isabella of Castile, the Kingdom of Castile, Navarra, The Canaries and all the territories of the Indies.

His great worry as a leader was keeping the Empire together, preventing it from dividing and for all those countries he inherited, which were very different and disparate, to have something in common that would unite them. Christianity and the catholic religion was a common unifying element he used to achieve this unity. However, this endeavour was not easy; by the contrary, it was specifically in his central European domains where Luther's Protestant Revolution was born, which ended up causing the great fall of the Catholic Church and the dividing of religious believers. This caused Charles to expend a great deal of energy trying to keep his subjects united. Also his foreign policy did not help him in this endeavour with continuous wars throughout his life waged against France and the Turks.

Regarding Spain, it took him a long time to earn the respect and approval of the Spanish people; it was not easy. Charles was considered too young and inexperienced as well as a foreigner who did not even know how to speak Spanish, nor had he ever lived in the country; he had been educated in the Netherlands, as per central European customs and beliefs. Even his brother Ferdinand who was educated here was favoured by his grandfather Ferdinand and by Castilians for succession. However and given the power and great inheritance that he could potentially unite, his grandfather, in his last will named him his successor with rights to all the Spanish crowns and their possessions, which also included those of his grandmother Isabella, who had died a few years back. He did not hold this right alone; he shared it with his mother. However, since his grandmother had been incapacitated due to a mental disease and had been interned in the castle of Tordesillas, it was the young Charles who held all the power and governance.

When Ferdinand the Catholic died in 1516, the young prince became Charles I of Spain. Charles did not come to Spain until September 1517, surrounded by a Flemish court, with whom he intended to use as collaborators and councilmen to govern here. This clumsy arrival earned him the mistrust and opposition of the Spanish people. This circumstance was aggravated by the fact that once the different courts of his kingdoms vowed him obedience, he left the country to take care of urgent matters in other European territories. In his absence, he appointed his Flemish collaborators to the highest government positions in Spain. These were years of great revolts and protests in the different kingdoms of Spain against their new king.

Charles I returned in 1522 as Emperor Charles V, after having inherited the imperial crown from his grandfather Maximilian of Habsburg. This time he stayed in Spain for quite a few years and made an effort to understand its culture. He learned how to speak Spanish and appointed Spaniards to the most important government positions. He slowly began to feel a profound love for Spain, which in some way radically changed the perception that Spaniards had of him here, earning him the respect of the people.

On 11 March 1526 in Seville he married his cousin princess Isabella of Portugal, who was of Spanish descent since she was also the granddaughter of the Catholic Kings. During his wedding trip he visited some of the most important cities of the country, which once again earned him the affection of the Spanish people. It was precisely by reason of this trip that he visited Granada and was surprised by the beauty of the Alhambra and this city, which had so been desired by his grandparents, the Catholic Kings. For this reason after his visit he ordered building a great palace in the Alhambra itself, which would be named after him.

In 1955, after having lived an intense life, tired and defeated in his effort to keep the empire together, he abdicated in his son Philip and his brother Ferdinand, dividing the most important territories between them. The title of emperor and the territories associated with the German Empire was left to the later. The Netherlands, Spain, the Indies and the possessions in Italy were passed on to Philip. In 1557 he retired to rest, meditate in God and prepare for death in the monastery of Yuste in Caceres. He died there on the 21st of September of 1558.

The Palace of Charles V

When Charles V came to Granada in 1526, he decided to build a Renaissance palace in the Alhambra itself, a palace that would come to be known as the "New Royal House."

When Charles V came to Granada on his honeymoon trip with Empress Isabel of Portugal in 1526, he stayed in the Alhambra, astonished by its beauty and that of the city. For this reason, he ordered the construction of a palace in the heart of the Alhambra, a palace that would be a worthy dwelling for the Emperor of the Holy Roman Empire and which would express the triumph of Christianity over Islam.

Main façade of the Palace of Charles V

Charles V assigned this task to the Marquis of Mondéjar, Governor of the Alhambra. Building began in 1527 under the direction of the architect Pedro Machuca, who had worked in Italy as a disciple of Miguel Ángel. In 1550, Machuca died and his son Luis continued the project, followed by Juan de Orea (now during the reign of Philip II), advised by Juan de Herrera (architect of the Monastery of El Escorial).

Detail of the Palace's bossage façade

From the start, the major funding for the construction came from the taxes collected from the Moriscos of Granada; their rebellion and subsequent expulsion complicated the project's continuation. Difficulties persisted with the ensuing financial crises and general indifference shown by the Spanish kings over the years. So great was the neglect and lack of resources that the palace remained without a roof until 1929.

The building's design was inspired by the classic formulas of Greco-Roman antiquity, symbol of power and perfection, recovered from the Italian Renaissance. The tremendous grandeur of the palace is truly striking in comparison with the humble scale of Nasrid buildings. The most important

Detail of the pediment of the gate on the south façade

Detail of one of the medallions on the main façade

Bas-relief on a pedestal of the ornamental columns along the main façade

Upper gallery of the Palace

façades are the southern and western ones. Their exteriors stand out, as does the decorative distinction between its two sections, lower and upper.

The lower section is made of dressed stone, Tuscan-style. The upper section displays details from a Late Renaissance tradition, with Ionic-style pediments and cornices on its windows. The southern frontispiece granted access to the Empress's chambers and is decoratively different from the western frontispiece, which allows access to the Emperor's palatine zone, the main façade, and the palace entrance.

Particularly notable are the four marble bas-reliefs on the pedestals of the columns along this main façade, which depict scenes from the Battle of Pavia, allegories of triumph and of the peace brought about by the war's end, cherubs holding up the world with the imperial crown, the Pillars of Hercules... The drawings on these reliefs were done by Machuca and the marble engraved by Juan de Orea and Leval.

Perhaps the most novel and surprising element for its time was the shape chosen for the floor, which inserts a circular court into a square-shaped building: two simple, perfect geometric forms. Inside, the austerity of the court is startling, as is the simplicity of its columns on both floors: the lower floor with 31 Doric-style columns and the upper with Ionic-style columns. The court wasn't finished exactly as Machuca had conceived it.

The palace houses two important museums. The Museo de la Alhambra (Museum of the Alhambra), with a collection of Nasrid art, is a required stop for understanding the daily life of the Alhambra's inhabitants. The Museo de Bellas Artes (Museum of Fine Arts) contains paintings and sculptures from the famous Granadian baroque school (seventeenth to eighteenth centuries) and from the modern age.

Circular court and double gallery inside the Palace

The Water of the Alhambra: La Acequia Real (The Royal Canal)

When Mohammed I (al-Ahmar) was planning to build his palace on the outskirts of Granada, on the Sabika hill, the Alhambra became know not just as a fortress, but also as a palatine city; one of the first projects that had to be undertaken was to bring water to this location. The Sabika was separated from the city by the Darro River, which was at its feet, at a much lower elevation than that of the city. Some studies maintain that centuries ago a hydraulic structure may have existed for the purpose of bringing water from this river to the Sabika, although clear archaeological evidence of this has not been discovered. However, it has been proven that it was the construction of the Acequia Rey (King Canal), also known as the Acequia Real (Royal Canal) by Almahar, during the first half of the XIII century, which enabled to irrigate the land and made this entire plan viable.

The water channel took water from the dam, which was built in the Darro River, six kilometres upstream from the Alhambra. The river was born at that location and routed the water to the Cerro del Sol (Hill of the Sun), where the Generalife was located, an agricultural area that supplied the entire palatine city, which was comprised of a hill and 4 large vegetable gardens. Three of them were at the same level as the water channel (Colorá, Grande and Fuentepeña) and the other one was at a higher elevation (la Mercería). From the Generalife, the water channel was routed to the Alhambra through an aqueduct that was built above the Aikibía ravine (currently called Cuesta de los Chinos) that separated the southern hillside of the Cerro del Sol from the Sabika hill.

At first the Royal Canal was only used for the land that surrounded its passage. Little by little a system of junctions and channels were incorporated, which allowed increasing the surface it irrigated. Even a sophisticated system was devised to bring the water from the water channel to the land located way above the elevation where said water was being routed, on the upper hillsides of the property. This was achieved via the construction of the Albercones (pools); structures that allowed storing water at the highest points, from where it was distributed, thus increasing the land available for cultivation.

The first pool that was built and the largest is Las Damas (The Ladies), which is located above the Generalife Palace (still exists today). Using a complex hydraulic system, part of the water from the water channel was rerouted through a large underground channel, to a deep well. The bottom of this well was even at a lower elevation than that of the water channel itself. The well filled with water from the bottom up. At its opening, way above, at the top of the hillside, there was a water wheel that was turned using animals and allowed bringing the water up from the well and fill the Las Damas reservoir. This hydraulic project allowed cultivating the land that was located above the

Royal Canal, as is the case of the Huerta de la Mercería.

At the start of the XV century, this system was improved through the construction of a new and more ambitious hydraulic project: The splitting of the Royal Canal three kilometres from its origin using a divider that divided the course of the channel into a second branch, the Acequia del Tercio (One Third of the Waterway) (called this way because it was the proportion of water that was derived from the first). The Royal Canal (which from then on was also known as the "Two Thirds") irrigated the lands that were located below and the "Third", which has a much shorter slope, ran through the land located at higher elevations. The water from this second channel also allowed supplying water to the Albercones without having to use the wheel. Once the land that was located at higher elevations was irrigated, the water left over from the Acequia del Tercio was routed to the Royal Canal, which increased its flow prior to it entering the Alhambra. The aqueduct used to bring water into the citadel was protected by the Water Tower, which had been built next to it in the sector located at the eastern end of the wall.

AQUEDUCT OF THE ROYAL CANAL AND WATER TOWER

Through this aqueduct, water flowed from the Generalife to the Alhambra. It was protected by the Tower, from which the canal was guarded so no one could sabotage the water supply — so important to the citadel's needs.

Today, many centuries later, that Royal Canal, which was built by al-Ahmar in the XIII century, is still functional, irrigating all the gardens and forests of the Alhambra.

The Generalife

A palace and leisure estate, stocked with gardens and hunting lands and independent of the Alhambra, the Generalife was used by the Nasrid kings as a place for rest and retreat.

The Generalife was a leisure estate, independent of the Alhambra, used by Nasrid kings as a place for rest and recreation. If we define the Alhambra as we know it today, it is difficult to grasp that the Granadan kings who lived there built — at such a short distance from their palaces, which were equipped with beautiful ponds, fountains and gardens — yet another palace and gardens designed for serenity. We must not forget that their palaces, no matter how beautiful they were, were located inside a walled enclosure: part of a complex, bustling city with many inhabitants, a city that accommodated the court, the administration of its political affairs, and the smooth operation of the Kingdom of Granada.

Viewed this way, it is much easier to understand the raison d'être of this beautiful palace surrounded by gardens and orchards that stocked the Alhambra. It occupied a much greater area than it does today, extending all the way out to the neighboring mountains. It was conceived to fulfill various

The Palace of the Generalife and its surroundings

functions: leisure, agriculture, cattle-raising, and hunting grounds. Today, the most widely accepted interpretation of its name is that it comes from the Arabic words *Yannat al-Arif*, meaning "garden of the architect."

Following the Christian conquest, the Generalife maintained its independence from the Alhambra. The Catholic Monarchs kept it as a separate municipality. In the Christian era, it was the personal property of the Granada-Villegas family. Since then, it has remained in private hands until 1921, when, after a long dispute, it became state property. In this new phase, its configuration underwent a dramatic transformation: in what used to be orchards, romantic gardens were built, incorporating fountains, water jets, trimmed shrubbery, cypress trees, and ornamentation more closely resembling the style of the typical Granadan villas-with-gardens — which soon came to resemble the rustic, agricultural style, or that of the Hispano-Muslim gardens of the past.

THE GENERALIFE

Drawing by Carlos Quintanilla

1. *Ampitheater*
2. *New Gardens*
3. *Colorá Orchard*
4. *Access patios to the Palace*
5. *South Pavilion*
6. *Court of the Canal*
7. *North Pavilion*
8. *Court of the Sultana*
9. *High Gardens*
10. *Romantic Observation Point*
11. *Water Ponds*
12. *Promenade of the Cypresses*

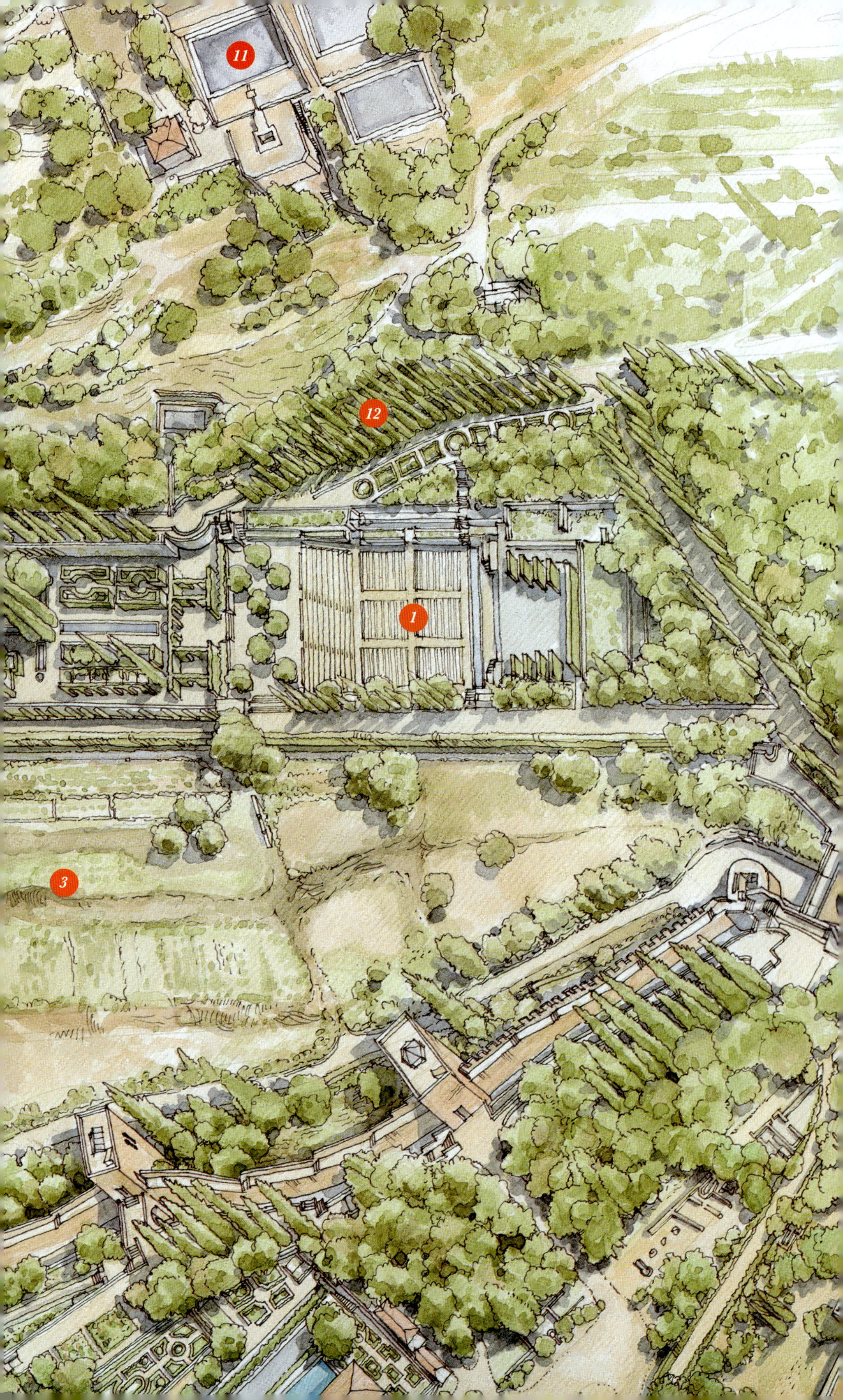
11
12
1
3

New Gardens
Jardines Nuevos

These gardens were one of the major modifications made to the estate after it became state property. In the medieval era, this entire area was filled with orchards, which supplied the Alhambra. There were at least three (Merecía, Colorá, Grande, and Fuentepeña). Most of them have disappeared or were urbanized through these New Gardens.

Fountain beside the pool of the New Gardens

Pool of the New Gardens

Part of one of the orchards still remains, however — the Colorá — which helps us imagine what this space might have been like during the Nasrid era.

The New Gardens were built in multiple sections. Cypresses predominate, trimmed into walls and labyrinths, as do pergolas and rose bushes. There is also an amphitheater, recently remodeled, which was built in 1952 for the concerts and performances of the Festival Internacional de Música y Danza de Granada and which is still used for this purpose. The central part contains a pool, with alternating fountains and cypresses, where water lilies float. In front and to the left, beautiful views of the Alhambra and the city crown the entire space.

The Albaicín and the Generalife orchards from the New Gardens

Palace of the Generalife

Palacio del Generalife

This palace is the core of the entire site. Undergoing transformations over the years, it was an authentic royal residence in the Muslim era, with all commodities and elements necessary for the visits of the Granadian kings.

The palace is accessed through two adjacent courts: the first is called the Patio del Descabalgamiento (Court of the Dismount) because the Nasrid emirs came from the Alhambra on horseback and dismounted here; hence the supports provided for this purpose, as well as a trough. The next court is a beautiful space adorned with orange trees and a fountain in the middle. In this court, a rectangular door with a tiled green and black lintel against a white background grants us entry to the palace.

Court preceding the Palace

Entrance gates to the Palace

Court of the Main Canal, south pavilion

Central viewpoint, in the west wing, of the Court of the Main Canal.

Corner of the Court of the Main Canal

General view of the Court of the Main Canal and the north pavilion

Royal Hall

Once inside, the central nucleus of the palace is the Court of the Main Canal. This is the most beautiful part of the precincts and one of the most famous gardens in the world. With two pavilions on its north and south sides, it is traversed by the Royal Canal and open to the landscape through the gallery of arches in the west wing. This gallery is a Christian modification, since, in medieval times, this side of the court was closed off by a wall; the only opening to the outside was the central look out, which conserved the rich decoration and low windows characterizing the Nasrid architecture and lifestyle. This wing is new; a fire in 1958 destroyed it almost completely.

The water jets on either side of the pool are not originals, either; they were incorporated in the nineteenth century and transformed the silent, whispering water of the Muslim canal into a sonorous stream.

Of the court's two pavilions, the northern one is the more interesting. Designed to be the king's chambers, it presents a traditional layout with a five-arched portico and adjacent bedrooms; the central arch is much wider than the side ones. This large central arch grants access to a triple-arched façade that precedes the royal hall and Ismail I's observation point. The rich, abundant decoration of its stucco work invites us to ponder the importance and wealth of the person who would have enjoyed the views from this lookout. The upper floors of the pavilion were a Christian extension in 1494.

Ismail I's Observation Point in the north pavilion

Court of the Sultana's Cypress Tree

Water jets in the Court of the Sultana's Cypress Tree

This pavilion is connected to the PATIO DEL CIPRÉS DE LA SULTANA (Court of the Sultana's Cypress Tree), now highly altered. This part of the palace bears no resemblance to what it was like in medieval times. Almost all of its current elements are Christian. It bears this name because, according to legend, by the old cypress tree (now petrified) in the court, the sultan Abu al-Hasan Ali caught the sultana exchanging declarations of love with an Abencerrage gentleman: a discovery that would prompt the massacre of the members of this illustrious Granadian lineage. It presents a unique porticoed structure, built in 1584, and a U-shaped pool ringed with water jets. A small pool occupies the center with a fountain emerging from it. The sound of the water here is almost deafening.

Central fountain in the Court

High Gardens Jardines Altos

Fountain in the High Gardens

The gardens are accessed by passing through a gate adorned with two lions and the Mendoza shield in the Court of the Sultana's Cypress Tree, ascending some stairs. Romantic in style, they are located in an upper floor of the Palace of Generalife; the views from here are spectacular. The gardens contain magnolias, cypress trees, an enormous cedar tree, and fragrant plants like myrtles, jasmine bushes, and rose bushes. Perhaps the most remarkable

Gate of the High Gardens and Romantic Observation Point

Water Stairway

element is the stunning Escalera del Agua (Water Staircase), one of the few Nasrid features conserved in this area. Here, water flows in a torrent down the balustrades, which are hollow and were originally decorated with tiles. Sheltered by laurels and hazelnut trees, we walk in the presence of these verses by Lorca: "Balustrades of the moon where the water resounds." The stairway leads us toward the Mirador Romántico (Romantic Observation Point), built in 1836 by the estate's administrator. Some authors believe that, given its position, there was once a Nasrid oratory here.

The Paseo de las Adelfas (Promenade of the Oleanders) and the Paseo de los Cipreses (Promenade of the Cypress Trees) complete our walk towards the exit.

General Bibliography

Bermúdez López, Jesús. *La Alhambra y el Generalife. Guía oficial.* Madrid-Granada, TF Editores-Patronato de la Alhambra y el Generalife, 2010.

Díez Jorge, María Elena; Gómez-Moreno Calera, José Manuel; and Galera Andreu, Pedro A. *La Alhambra y el Generalife. Guía histórico-artística.* Granada, Universidad de Granada and Junta de Andalucía, 2006.

Hierro Calleja, Rafael. *Granada y la Alhambra.* Granada, Ediciones Miguel Sánchez, 2004.

Bermúdez Pareja, Jesús. "El baño del Palacio de Comares en la Alhambra de Granada. Disposición primitiva y alteraciones." *Cuadernos de la Alhambra,* n°s 10-11. Granada, Patronato de la Alhambra, 1974.

Irving, Washington. *Cuentos de la Alhambra.* Granada, Ediciones Miguel Sánchez, 1976.

Guillén, Rafael. *Granada. Invención del Aire.* Granada, Ediciones Miguel Sánchez, 2006.

García-Fresneda Martínez, Ángeles. *La Fórmula.* Granada, Ediciones Miguel Sánchez, 2009.

Villa-Real, Ricardo. *Homenaje a Granada. Selección de textos poéticos y literarios.* Granada, Ediciones Miguel Sánchez, 1990.

Monograph Bibliography

THE MUSLIM PEOPLES, MASTERS OF AL-ÁNDALUS (711-1429). Excerpted verbatim from: Hierro Calleja, Rafael. *Granada y la Alhambra.* Granada, Ediciones Miguel Sánchez, 2004.

THE CATHOLIC MONARCHS, ARCHITECTS OF THE UNITY OF THE SPANISH KINGDOMS. Excerpted verbatim from: Hierro Calleja, Rafael. *Granada y la Alhambra.* Granada, Ediciones Miguel Sánchez, 2004.

THE HISPANIC-MUSLIM HOME AND DOMESTIC LIFE. Orihuela Uzal, Antonio. *Casas y palacios nazaríes siglos XIII-XV.* Barcelona, Editorial Lunwerg, 1996.

DECORATION AND ORNAMENTATION (I): TECHNIQUES, RESOURCES AND DECORATIVE ELEMENTS OF ISLAMIC ARCHITECTURE. Excerpted verbatim from: Hierro Calleja, Rafael. *Granada y la Alhambra.* Granada, Ediciones Miguel Sánchez, 2004.

DECORATION AND ORNAMENTATION (II): MOST FREQUENT DECORATIVE THEMES AND MOTIFS. Excerpted verbatim from: Hierro Calleja, Rafael. *Granada y la Alhambra.* Granada, Ediciones Miguel Sánchez, 2004.

CHARLES V, THE GREAT WESTERN EMPEROR. http://www.biografiasyvidas.com

THE WATER OF THE ALHAMBRA: LA ACEQUIA REAL (THE ROYAL CANAL). Pérez Asensio, Manuel. "Intervención arqueológica en un tramo de la Acequia Real de la Alhambra." *Cuadernos de la Alhambra*, vol. 43. Granada, Patronato de la Alhambra y el Generalife, 2008.

SLOPE OF LOS CHINOS
Connection to the city (Albaicín)

GOMÉREZ SLOPE and ALHAMBRA WOODS
Connection to the city (Plaza Nueva)

PARTAL PROMENADE AND TOWERS →
Internal connection Alcazaba-Palaces with the Generalife

PATH OF THE SECANO ↔
Internal connection Generalife with Alcazaba-Palaces

A ***Entrance pavilion***
Access to the Generalife
Tickets

B ***Access to the Palaces***

C ***Access to the Alcazaba***

1 Gate of the Pomegranates
2 Pillar of Charles V
3 Gate of Justice
4 Wine Gate
5 Garden of the Defense Paths
6 Tower of the Pólvora
7 Bastion of the Darro
8 Tower of the Vela
9 Tower of the Hidalgos
10 Gate of Arms
11 Military District
12 Tower of Homage
13 Broken Tower
14 Tower of the Hens
15 Tower of Machuca
16 THE MEXUAR
17 PALACE OF COMARES
18 Tower of Comares
19 PALACE OF THE LIONS
20 CHRISTIAN ROOMS
21 Tower of the Ladies
22 Remnants of the Palace of Yusuf III
23 Tower of the Pointed Battlements
24 Tower of the Cadí
25 Tower of the Captive
26 Tower of the Infants
27 Tower of the Career Corporal
28 Water Tower
29 Tower of Juan de Arce
30 Tower of Baltasar de la Cruz
31 Gate of the Seven Floors
32 Tower of the Captain
33 Tower of the Witches
34 Remnants of Nasrid houses
35 Parador San Francisco
36 Tower of Heads
37 Remnants of the Palace of the Abencerrages
38 Saint Mary of the Alhambra Church
39 PALACE OF CHARLES V
40 Promenade of the Cypresses
41 Amphitheater
42 New Gardens
43 Colorá Orchard
44 PALACE OF THE GENERALIFE
45 High Gardens

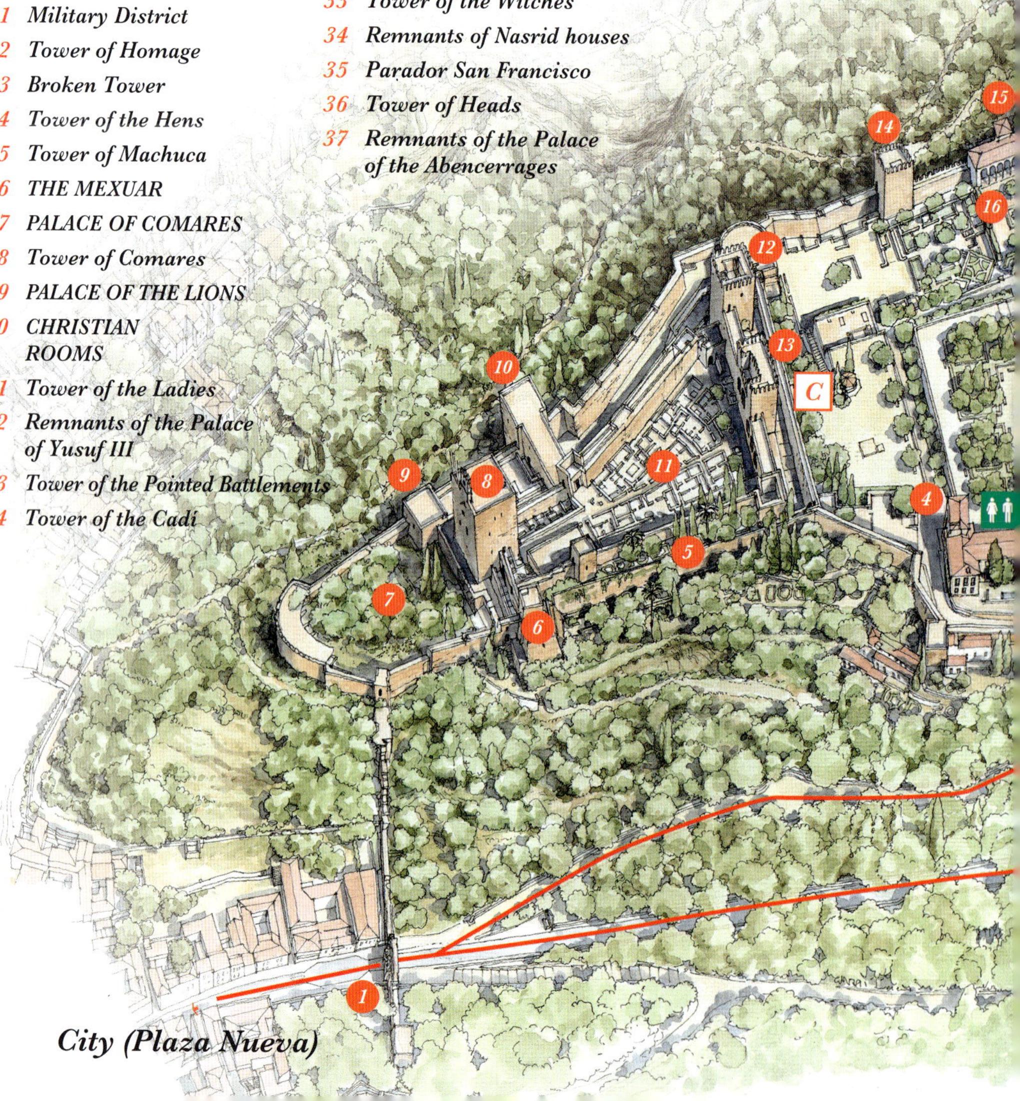

Drawing by Carlos Quintanilla